STOLEN SISTERS

A John Treehorn Mystery

Dinah Miller

Copyright © 2018 by Dinah Miller

New York Productions, LLC
P. O. Box 175
Churubusco, New York 12923

STOLEN SISTERS A John Treehorn Mystery is a work of fiction. Names, characters, places, and incidents are either the product of the author's imagination or are used fictitiously. Any resemblance to actual persons, living or dead, events, or locales is entirely coincidental.

ISBN 978-0-9979826-2-6 (EBook)
ISBN 978-0-9979826-3-3 (Paperback Edition)
ISBN 978-0-9979826-4-0 (Hardcover Edition)

Printed in the United States of America

Cover Artwork by Leonie Cheetham
www.facebook.com/leoniecheethamart

www.facebook.com/SpecialAgentJohnTreehorn

www.dinahmiller.com (Book orders and merchandise.)

To

Mia, Janis, Dana, Susan, and Annie.

It takes a village.

Death wears a red dress.

—FBI Special Agent John Treehorn

Chapter One

The brisk North Dakota prairie winds blew across the desolate fields and snow banks that lined the highway. Everything was gray-tinged in the early morning hours. The only movement, a hungry wolf whose shape appeared like a mirage as he wore his mangy fur coat.

The wolf smelled his prey at the same time he noticed the red dress swinging in the wind. He followed the scent to a freshly disturbed snow and gravel-covered shallow grave. His sharp nails dug at the contents until a pale, feminine hand with red-painted fingernails appeared, seeming to hold a crumb-filled bag. Inside were two items, a gold FBI badge and a yellow sticky note with five simple words written on it: *Call FBI Agent John Treehorn.* The frightened wolf ran, ran as if the devil named Treehorn was chasing him to hell and back.

Trooper Toby Allen, in a North Dakota Highway Patrol car, passed the wolf as it ran in the opposite direction past the *Leaving Lakken Oil Fields* sign. He slowed his car and activated his spotlight to examine the area. Something

1

had scared the wolf, an animal that wasn't easily spooked. The trooper searched the area and located the disturbed snow and gravel. The veteran officer's spotlight found the feminine hand protruding from the snowbank. There were no signs of footprints near the body other than the wolf's paw prints. The trooper stepped out of his warm cruiser to investigate, avoiding the two mud puddles. His flashlight illuminated the hand and the gold law enforcement badge. On closer inspection, he identified the badge as an FBI-issue. He wiped the snow from the face and recognized the deceased body from the ice-coated eyelids of her open eyes.

He called the local dispatcher with his handheld radio, "Car 1311, Trooper Allen here."

"Dispatch. Go ahead, 1311."

"We have a 10-79 at south mile marker two-two-four, past the town line."

"Can you repeat? Did you say *dead body*?" questioned the operator over the radio static.

"Yes, I repeat, a 10-79," Trooper Allen clarified, shaking his head. "Send the coroner and patch me through to the on-call FBI agent."

"Will do," dispatch stated.

Trooper Allen was grateful that a local agent would be calling the FBI director and not him. As he waited for dispatch, he saw headlights and watched as a Lakken Energy truck approached going well over the speed limit. It maneuvered and intentionally hit a large puddle splashing both the trooper and the dead body.

"Asshole," he muttered to himself as he recorded the truck's license plate number.

When he returned to his cruiser, soaked from head to toe, Trooper Allen sipped his coffee and asked himself two investigative questions: "Was the dead body the owner of the FBI badge and who in the hell was FBI Agent John Treehorn? Both answers, he would soon find, were way above his pay grade.

FBI Special Agent John Treehorn entered his office building through glass doors marked with the FBI insignia. The six-foot-tall American Indian, his short black hair cut to FBI regulation, walked with strength and determination, no sign of weakness at age thirty-five. He glanced at the red-dressed woman as she passed him in the hall. Some men would notice the beauty of her face, the full breasts, the long legs, or how the cut of the dress contoured to the shape of her body. Not Treehorn. He remembered his wife in her red dress, in the silk-lined, ivory casket on the day he buried her fifteen years earlier.

As always, his trusted administrator, Abby, was there to greet him, "Good morning, John."

"Good morning, Abby." He handed her a travel mug of coffee.

"You'll be the one needing the travel mug." Abby pointed to his packed suitcase by the door. "Boss needs to see you right now. If I don't see you before you leave, have a safe trip."

Treehorn leaned into Abby's personal space, where she took the opportunity to inhale his musky, sagely scent. "North Dakota," she whispered.

He nodded and strode down the corridor to his supervisor's office. It was rare that his bags were packed for him, but when they were, it was never a good sign. The agent greeted his supervisor's personal assistant, "Good morning, Patricia."

"Good morning, John. Go right in, he's expecting you."

Leo Mancuso was on the telephone with his boss, the FBI director.

Treehorn sat in an upholstered chair while Patricia closed the door.

"I'm sending Treehorn. He'll head the investigation," stated Mancuso. He listened to the director's reply and nodded, "I'll let him know." He ended the call.

"Good morning," Treehorn said.

"No, it's not," answered Mancuso. "That was the boss. That was the second call I received from him this morning. We have a dead body in North Dakota. It was found less than an hour ago holding an FBI badge with a note addressed to you." Mancuso handed Treehorn a police photo that showed red-painted fingernails grasping a plastic bag that held the message and gold shield.

"Whose badge?" Treehorn asked.

"Raven Shelly," Mancuso answered.

"Is he okay?" Treehorn asked, concerned. Raven Shelly was Treehorn's married friend and fellow agent assigned to the Navajo Indian Reservation.

"Yes, he's fine," Mancuso answered. "He's up there investigating a missing Navajo woman who disappeared in Williston a week ago, a Sandy Begay."

"Is this her?" Treehorn asked.

"No, this is a different woman. The director has a plane waiting for you at Reagan. It'll fly you out." Mancuso handed Treehorn the file. "Quantico assigned an indigenous, forensic medical examiner out there to assist the local coroner, Dr. William Ryder, a month ago. The preliminary autopsy should be completed by the time you arrive."

"Why me when you have local agents and LEOs already there?"

"They're swamped with all of the Lakken Energy Company personnel. All they do is cause chaos and mayhem. The director wants to know how an FBI agent misplaced his badge and why a dead woman would ask for you," Mancuso stated. "She is getting her request."

"Has the victim been identified?" Treehorn asked.

"She's one of your people," Mancuso answered.

"*My* people?" Treehorn questioned his boss's racial inference.

"Don't get your Indian underwear in a twist. She's Navajo, an engineer from your reservation. She carried an Arizona driver's license and was employed by Lakken Energy. Her name was Darcy Clearwater."

Treehorn would read up on the Clearwater family clan during his flight. He wasn't expected to know every person from his reservation. With a population of over 300,000 and covering 27,000 square miles, he would learn what he needed to know.

"Send me an update after you receive the coroner's preliminary report. I want to know how Agent Shelly's badge was found on a victim who he wasn't investigating," Mancuso ordered, "and tell him to give me a call after you interview him."

"Yes, sir," Treehorn answered. Two Navajo women, Agent Shelly had a missing woman, and now, within a week, there was a second woman, dead and holding his badge, in the same oil boomtown, hundreds of miles from the Rez. Treehorn knew foul play connected the two cases because he never believed in coincidences.

The first plane landed at the Minot Air Force Base and Treehorn transferred to a G-150 that had been confiscated from a felonious CEO. It flew him the remaining 120 miles to Williston, North Dakota. The airport had grown proportionally to the explosion of the oil and natural gas fields of the Lakken Energy Corporation; as had the crime. The FBI had opened a field office here to address the jurisdictional crimes that occurred when money flowed like water. Treehorn saw it, in crime after crime, how money and lawlessness always went hand in hand.

As he exited the plane, an FBI staff member was holding a package for the pilot, who accepted it with his signature. "Have a safe flight to Tucson. A staff member will be waiting for you when you land."

Treehorn took the time to watch the G-150 as it roared down the runway. The airport was a twenty-four seven hub of activity. Miles of metal pipe, neatly stacked, lined the perimeter, a testament to hardworking men and machinery for the oil and gas exploration in the area.

The employee knew Treehorn was with the FBI upon his arrival, "Welcome to Williston. You need a ride?"

"Thanks, but I have a car waiting."

Treehorn signed for his dark blue SUV vehicle that waited for him. He opened his folder, examined the local map, and headed to the location where the corpse and badge were found. The prairie stretched from horizon to horizon as Treehorn drove out of the airport parking lot. Sections of dead grass poked through the snow-covered ground. The daylight hours were fading fast in the winter afternoon, making his time short to inspect a body dump location.

He drove the back roads to get a feel for the land. The *Entering Lakken Energy Fields* sign separated the prairie from the oil and natural gas rigs that dotted the skyline. Treehorn parked his vehicle and surveyed the location. He opened the file and re-examined the report. The body had been found buried in fresh snow with some gravel. He stepped out of the vehicle and crossed the ditch where the stream flowed toward the prairie and away from the town. The yellow police ribbon fluttered in the wind, its brightness a sharp contrast against the pristine surroundings. A single tree, surrounded by the harsh prairie and oil wells, somehow survived life in the North Dakota winters. A red dress, attached to the tree's branch, swung gently in the breeze and waved as if to say, "Here I am, please don't ignore me." Treehorn examined the area. Why would someone hang a red dress in a tree and dump a body here? He walked the perimeter and went to the other side of the erected sign which read, *Leaving Lakken Energy Fields.* The weather had faded and washed away parts of the letters.

Darcy Clearwater, Navajo, age thirty-two, was dumped in the middle of nowhere, far from town, and without a witness in sight. He didn't know why the victim was holding a note with *Call FBI Agent John Treehorn* scribbled across it. He didn't know the victim or her family. They lived near Lake Powell, an area in the northwestern edge of the Navajo Indian Reservation.

He examined the crime scene photos on his phone: the body placement near the ditch, the note with the badge in her hand, the distance from the tree, and the red dress that hung in the tree. He snapped a few more pictures of the single tree and lone dress. The red material formed an eerie backdrop against the leafless winter tree and the freshly fallen snow. He wondered why the crime scene unit technicians had left the dress hanging there. Again, he examined the dress in the crime photo, then looked at the one blowing in the wind, and realized they weren't the same.

Treehorn memorized the area before returning to his vehicle. As winter faded, the tree would grow, and the water would flow clear with its spring rains. All signs of Darcy's death would be washed away. He glanced one last time at the gray, dismal prairie that spread out on one side of the Lakken sign and the energy rigs that were on the other. In the distance, the energy wells and the town's lights created a golden haze in the early evening skyline. Treehorn secured his paperwork in his SUV and drove towards the town.

He passed the Lakken-owned housing projects. Hundreds of trailers lined up to answer the needs of the workers known as frackers. North Dakota State Troopers, the FBI, and the DEA were busy patrolling the area in their law enforcement vehicles, with red and blue lights flashing. They were interviewing witnesses and handcuffing men who did wrong, which appeared to be a twenty-four seven operation. The men's public drunkenness and the women's solicitations weren't a focus of law enforcement; serious crimes of assault, kidnapping, and murder appeared to be the norm. He drove past the housing on the newly-paved, two-lane highway that merged into the one-light town.

Treehorn parked his SUV in a slushy parking spot on Main Street and checked his GPS. An Indian with dyed red hair knocked on his car window; her profession identified her by her black leather dress, fishnet stockings, and thigh-high, black leather boots. He lowered his window. The whiff of her expensive perfume combined with the petroleum odor outside wasn't a pleasant combination. The woman's face showed the skin of someone in her early twenties, but her eyes spoke a different story. She placed her business card in his jacket breast pocket.

"Are you passing through, half-breed? Need some company?"

"What's your name?" Treehorn asked the young woman.

"It can be anything you want it to be."

"Is it on your business card?"

"Just my number." When she smiled, her teeth sparkled and Treehorn suspected a large chunk of her change had paid for premium dental services.

"Okay, *Just My Number*, I'm sorry, but I can't accept your request for company." Treehorn showed her his FBI badge beneath his jacket.

"That hasn't stopped others," she said matter-of-factly through chewing gum, which probably wasn't dentist recommended.

Treehorn squinted and frowned with displeasure.

"FBI agents?" he asked as he covered his badge.

"Your badges all look alike," she flippantly answered.

"How about my handcuffs?" Treehorn asked.

"Now, there's no reason to show me yours. I'm just trying to pay my water bill."

Treehorn removed one of his business cards from his pocket and wrote on the back. "Here's my card. If you have any names of police and their badge numbers, you can use that for your time in need, like a get out of a jail card, Just My Number."

She examined his card, "You never know when this may come in handy in my line of work, Mr. G-man," she tucked it into her bra cup.

"Can you point me toward the Williston Community Hospital?"

"Take a right at the light, a mile down the road, on the right."

"You be safe, Just My Number."

"You too, and if you change your mind, this is my watering hole."

Treehorn read the blue neon sign: THIRSTY'S.

"The self-righteous town council wouldn't let them put beer on the sign since it was across from the church."

He observed the town, or more precisely the two towns. One side of the street had several bars and honky-tonks, the other side had simple white churches. One appeared for the oil and gas workers, the other for the townsfolk who tried to eke out a basic living.

"You take care."

Treehorn glanced in his rearview mirror as he drove away from the revelry and saw Just My Name had already found another john.

The foggy drizzle continued en route to the hospital. Residents huddled under umbrellas in an attempt to stay dry. Neat little houses lined one side of the street while locally owned grocers, plumbing, and electrical stores lined the other. Treehorn followed the blue and white hospital sign and parked in the visitor parking lot. Even a mile away, the sounds of the honky-tonk's music reverberated as he exited his vehicle. The street lamp reflected his gold FBI badge onto the exterior of the dark blue SUV. It didn't let him forget why he was here and neither did the single red dress swinging from the utility pole, an eerie sight for the town's newcomer.

Chapter Two

Williston Community Hospital

Treehorn entered the main door and found the elderly clerk, name-tagged *Hollis*, sleeping soundly and drooling on the sign-in log. The agent scribbled his name and the time. A directory map posted on the wall provided directions: *Morgue: Basement.* One flight of stairs led to a long, darkened hallway.

A janitor, with *Juan* on his name tag, wore headphones as his red, buffing-machine pad cleaned the dirty, wet floors to a spotless shine.

Treehorn stopped because he didn't want his shoes shined. He waved his badge, and the janitor spotted the stranger and shut off his machine.

Juan removed an ear bud to hear the man.

"Morgue?"

The Hispanic janitor pointed his aged, arthritic fingers toward the end of the hallway, "Last door on the right. Cleaning up someone's mess?"

Treehorn nodded, "Always." and clipped his badge back to his belt. His appreciation for the janitor increased as he heard Foreigner's *'Dirty White Boy'* blaring from the man's headset as he resumed his duties.

Treehorn walked down the corridor toward the illuminated door of the morgue. He hesitated before entering. Sometimes, it was the smell of disinfectant or the dead spirits that lingered, but this time it was the raised voices that caused his neck hairs to rise. The agent stepped into the room and stopped. Two men and a woman were present. One man wore a uniform of a North Dakota State Trooper and the other a disheveled suit.

The suit flirted with the red-headed medical examiner, "Come have a drink with me." The suit nodded toward the state trooper. "He's married."

"So, are you," the ME answered, "Trooper Allen. Go home to your wonderful wife, Roni. I'll have a report for you in the morning. I appreciate your dedication. As for you Agent Asshole, go home to your hand."

"Come on, I know you want me." The suit continued his sexual harassment.

Trooper Allen had heard enough. "Leave her alone, Donovan."

The ME asked the law officers, "Who's John Treehorn and why would the victim be holding a note asking to call him?"

Agent Donovan spoke up before the agent could speak. "Treehorn's some half-breed out of Washington. He may have known her from the Rez. I heard he likes to be called Treehorn. What's up with that?"

"Please leave, Agent Donovan," she ordered, as she covered the body. "I want someone here who'll find this woman's killer."

"I will." The three professionals' attention snapped to the morgue entrance.

Agent Donovan spoke first: "Hey buddy, this is a restricted area. I'm FBI. You need to leave." He pointed to the door.

Treehorn's eyes met the ME's green eyes. "I'll help you," he said while he ignored Agent Donovan.

The ME gazed at the tall, handsome stranger, and thought: *I'll take your help.*

Donovan walked towards Treehorn.

Treehorn opened his suit and displayed his service weapon to the agent. This stopped the suit in his tracks and forced his hand to his own gun. Treehorn opened his other side of his jacket and showed his FBI badge.

17

Donovan stared at the man's brown-blue heterochromia eyes, "Who are you?"

"I'm that half-breed from Washington." Treehorn spoke with a calmness that made Trooper Allen move.

Donovan's face flushed from winter pale to summer sunburn. "Hey, I'm sorry," he stammered.

"Sorry for what?" challenged Treehorn as he stared down the man. He had a good six inches over Agent Donovan, whose face turned a deeper shade of crimson. Treehorn had heard every bigoted and racist comment known to man slung at him about his heritage since he was old enough to understand the white man's language. His red skin usually ignored it, but today he felt the medical examiner's eyes on him, felt an attraction, and felt he had betrayed his wife's spirit.

The state trooper stepped in front of the humiliated agent before the Indian smashed Agent Donovan's face into the next day. He offered his hand to Agent Treehorn. "Trooper Toby Allen. I found the body."

Treehorn shook his hand and gave him a professional nod. "John Treehorn."

Allen and Treehorn stepped around Donovan.

The ME removed her latex gloves and anticipated the touch of the agent's hand. "Dr. Samantha Reynolds." She eyed his left hand and saw his wedding ring. That put the brakes on her foolishness. She immediately knew this man was different when she met his glance. His irises were brown on the outer edge with an inner blue shade. The doctor in her became curious.

"FBI Special Agent John Treehorn." He glanced at her left hand as he presented his ID.

Agent Donovan found his voice. "I'll leave you to the investigation."

The agent hadn't taken two steps when Treehorn spoke, "If you wish to file a sexual harassment complaint against him, I'll write it up." Treehorn knew his voice carried the length of the room.

Allen tag-teamed, "I'll witness it."

The three heard Agent Donovan's hasty retreat. He offered no apology, and no one expected one.

The doctor threw her gloves into a trash can, "Women face harassment here every day, in one form or another. This whole area breeds contempt. There's definitely something in the water." The ME stepped off her soapbox, "This town asked for help and the help sent me."

"The offer stands." Treehorn's voice was a soothing salve.

"Thank you, but I didn't reach my pay grade by stepping on assholes."

"Touché." Treehorn smiled.

Trooper Allen interrupted the two, "I'm heading home. I'll read your report tomorrow, Dr. Reynolds. Agent Treehorn. Good luck with your investigation."

"Trooper Allen, how did you find the body in the middle of nowhere?" Treehorn delayed the officer's departure.

The officer thought of the wolf, and the agent saw his hesitation. "Someone marked my patrol car with 'MM 224.' That mile marker is in my patrol area and I decided to investigate."

Treehorn asked for clarification, "How was your car marked?"

"Someone scratched the ice on the driver's side window. I didn't see who. There were no witnesses or surveillance in the area."

Treehorn accepted his explanation. The marking meant there was a local who witnessed the body dump and possibly the identification of the killer.

"If you're looking for Agent Shelly, he was over at the Painted Pony Diner. It's across from the tower."

Treehorn shook his hand again. "Thanks."

The morgue got awkwardly quiet after the trooper departed. The clock hands clicked.

"I never noticed how loud that clock is." The doctor flushed and laughed with embarrassment.

Treehorn offered a small smile until he saw her wedding ring flash in the overhead light. His telltale facial shift disappeared. This was a line he had never crossed because it had never appeared. He focused on the case.

The doctor watched the agent's professional side re-emerge. Her respect for the man grew.

"What did you find, Doc?"

"I faxed the body dump location images to the FBI. You received them, right?"

Treehorn nodded, "I visited the site when I arrived and wondered why someone had placed a body there."

"We may never know." The doctor grabbed her file and set out to impress the married FBI agent. "Darcy Clearwater, age thirty-two, born on the Navajo Indian Reservation, a geologist for Lakken Energy. Cause of death was asphyxiation due to blunt force trauma. Someone struck her on the right zygomatic bone, aka right cheekbone, with a left-handed closed fist; it wasn't a fatal blow. It did leave a ring impression, plain band, and bruising, but not enough detail to identify. She fell and

21

struck a rounded object at the back of her head, fracturing her C4 vertebra which led to asphyxiation. Whatever she fell on may have trace blood on it because she had a small laceration from the object." The doctor showed Treehorn images of a circular bruise pattern. The coroner continued, "Postmortem lividity shows blood pooled in her tissues. This tells me she died in the prone position with her head turned outwards. She watched her killer as she died. She did have sex prior to her death and was sodomized postmortem. I sent semen samples to the lab. We have a necrophiliac psychopath on our hands. Someone washed her body postmortem and scrubbed it clean. They wanted no evidence left on the outside of the body. I took a water sample from her lungs for testing."

"Is it possible there were two killers? One wanted the body scrubbed of his involvement and the other didn't care?"

"Possible. Something may show up on the routine blood and tissue samples I sent to the lab. She has a tattoo on her ring finger; it's random markings in a circle. It's a unique, personal tribal marking, like nothing I've seen before. It had been covered by an actual ring which was missing."

Treehorn examined the tattoo photo. "Personal effects?"

They moved to a separate table where labeled, plastic evidence bags lined the table.

The ME touched each bag as she focused on its contents. "One red purse was found with the body. It contained her wallet, Arizona driver's license, credit cards, cash, lipstick, a ticket stub, and a set of keys. What's missing?"

"Her phone," Treehorn guessed.

"Yes! The crime scene unit is processing her apartment; it's the murder location. The apartment didn't appear to be a primary residence, so where was she living? Her Jeep was also parked there, so I had it towed to our garage. The lab will process it tomorrow after the apartment."

"Okay." Treehorn examined the key ring in the evidence bag. It contained a Jeep key, two basic silver house keys, a blue, office logo key, a brass post office key, and one other.

"She was wearing a smashed watch. It was filled with snow, and part of the watch crystal was missing. If the watch wasn't tampered with, it could be her time of death.

Because the body was in the snowbank, I can only give an estimated time of death."

The agent examined the very unusual and expensive watch through the evidence bag. Engraved on the back of the watch was the word: *Forever*. "This was a gift given to her by someone who loved her." Treehorn rubbed the bag that covered the watch with sadness. Her time was up.

"The watch had GPS, so I'm requesting a printout. Her left wrist sustained an impact fracture beneath the watch. Someone stomped on it as she lay dying; two of her fingers were also fractured." The ME moved down the table of evidence. "We have the red dress she was found in and her red Jimmy Choo shoes."

Treehorn examined the items. He noticed the colors didn't match and dress label sewn into the collar identified a cheap manufacturer.

"Do you notice that something is off?"

"The dress doesn't match the expensive shoes."

The ME laid her hand on top of the plastic evidence bag that Treehorn held. "This isn't her dress. This is a cotton dress and not her size."

Treehorn examined the dress through the plastic bag.

"I found blood soaked into the hem. It may have been from a cut from the original owner. It wasn't washed.

I found hair samples, epithelial cells, sweat, and cheap perfume." The ME theorized, "The killer re-dressed her…"

Treehorn concluded, "…in another woman's clothing."

"Not just anyone's."

"Whose?" Treehorn questioned.

"It matches the clothing description of Agent Shelly's missing woman, Sandy Begay. I sent DNA samples to the University of Arizona lab. They'll have the results by morning."

The ME wanted to kiss him and felt lightheaded because of it. He was handsome and smart.

Dr. Reynolds touched another red dress. "The Missing and Murdered Indigenous Women's movement hung this one in the tree. Have you seen the red dresses hanging around the community?"

"Yes, on the drive here. There was a dress hanging in the tree this afternoon when I examined the body dump location."

"The MMIW movement may have hung another one there out of respect for the victim. It's to remind us that all of the victims aren't forgotten."

"It's sad they have to do that," Treehorn sympathized.

Samantha nodded. "There was no underwear on this victim." The coroner glanced at Treehorn's belt. His eyes met hers and he watched as the blush covered her face.

The agent didn't joke. "He could have kept the underwear as a trophy."

"That's a theory, or she went without." Treehorn gave her an intense look and Samantha felt her face redden again.

"Agent Shelly was here earlier to see if this woman was his missing person. I explained the details of the red dress." She sought the next evidence bag as Treehorn returned the bags to the table. "Last item, one bag, contained three items." She held up three evidence bags: one containing Agent Shelly's FBI badge, the next the yellow note with *Call FBI Agent John Treehorn* written in cursive, and the last holding the plastic bag that had contained the badge and note. "This bag and items were found tucked into Darcy's hand, not inside her purse. I don't believe the killer left these items on the body. I believe a witness did after the fact."

"Why do you think that?" Treehorn's investigative mind had assumed that based on Trooper Allen's reporting but was interested in her hypothesis.

"Fingerprints. The FBI badge had two sets of fingerprints on it; one set was Agent Shelly's; the other prints were partials and not in the system."

"They didn't match the victim's?"

The medical examiner shook her head. "The writing on the yellow note matched Darcy's. Her company sent over a handwriting sample earlier today. Her fingerprints were on the note, and there were more partials matching the unknown ones like on the badge."

Treehorn examined the last bag that contained the plastic baggie.

"The bag contained one set of fingerprints. The same print was on the badge, note, and baggie. If you identify them, you'll know who left the badge and the note on the body. It means you have a witness to a crime," Dr. Reynolds deducted.

"Who could possibly identify the killer? They knew where the body was dumped and, now, that person's life may be in danger. The same person knew the victim and knew she wanted me here. Maybe, that's why they stole Shelly's badge and planted it on the body with the note." Treehorn could tell that the ME had one more question and wanted to know why she hesitated in asking. "Are you going to ask?"

"Did you know her? Is that why she asked for you?"

Treehorn stared at the Irish coroner; her curly, red hair framed a heart-shaped face with sparkling green eyes; freckles adorned her pale skin. She was smart and beautiful. He broke eye contact and examined the victim's driver's license photo. His wedding band shone brightly under the morgue's lights. "I didn't know her, and I don't know why she wanted me called, but I'll do my best to find the answer."

"I admire that, someone who speaks for the victim. Sometimes I think I'm the only one, Agent Treehorn," Dr. Samantha Reynolds answered matter-of-factly.

"Please, call me Treehorn."

"If you call me Samantha."

He nodded and removed an official paper from his breast pocket. "Here's permission for you to release Agent Shelly's badge to me if you're done with it."

Samantha removed the badge from the evidence bag. As she reached for the paper, their hands collided, and she dropped the FBI badge. They bent over to retrieve it and their heads bumped. They both gave embarrassed chuckles. Treehorn grabbed the badge; the ME snatched the paper.

The agent handed her his business card, "Here's my contact information. I'm staying at the FBI housing. Can you leave the watch and the specifics of the dress out the preliminary report for now?"

"Yes, but why?"

"The killer made three mistakes: dressing her in the wrong dress and stomping on her wrist. I would prefer people to focus on the fact she died from blunt force trauma," Treehorn requested.

The coroner nodded.

"Who identified the body?"

The coroner examined the documentation. "Robert Beltram, II. He's her supervisor at Lakken Energy. They've offered to pay for all expenses, including transporting of the body to the Navajo Indian Reservation, for burial."

Treehorn frowned as the memory of his own wife's burial on the Rez resurfaced.

"Thank you, Samantha."

Treehorn offered her his hand to shake. He wanted to feel the softness of her hand one last time. She watched Treehorn as he closed his eyes briefly as if to memorize her touch. She felt the same way.

"What was the killer's third mistake?" Samantha asked.

"I'm here to hunt him down," Treehorn answered.

The janitor coughed from the doorway.

The agent and the doctor jumped apart.

"Thank you, Agent Treehorn."

As Treehorn passed the janitor, he heard Adam Freeland's remix of Sarah Vaughan's *"Fever"* emanating from the man's headphones.

The janitor nodded to the Fed as he passed and asked the doctor, "You okay, Doc?"

She waved a paper in front of her face, "I'm feeling hot."

The janitor watched the long-legged FBI agent stride away. "Let me know when you need me to walk you to your car."

"Thanks, Juan."

Hollis, the sign-out man, watched as Treehorn wrote his departure time in the log. "Thanks for coming."

"You take care." Treehorn raised the collar of his jacket as he left the hospital, but it offered little protection against the frigid North Dakota breeze sweeping the parking lot. The red dress, tethered to the utility pole, danced gracefully in the wind, almost as if its spirit waved to him for his attention.

The Navajo agent couldn't prevent the chill that crept up his spine.

Chapter Three

Treehorn drove past the honky-tonks where cash-rich oil field workers partied, past weary-eyed local residents who avoided the revelers, and red dresses that swung from the utility poles en route to the Painted Pony Diner and Agent Raven Shelly. He located the restaurant with its neon lights that were fashioned like a pony and the silver-sided train car illuminated by the lights. It wasn't hard to locate it in the one-horse town. All the buildings were only one or two stories tall and the Williston Water Tower stood a hundred feet higher than every building in town.

He entered the window-lined diner and, with his ingrained law enforcement background and did a threat assessment of the varied selection of the people of the township. The townspeople sat on one side of the diner and the oil-energy employees the other. The patterned, black-and-white checkered floor told everyone everything was made to appear black and white.

Samuel Bear, age 60, police chief of the Navajo Nation Police Department and Treehorn's lifelong friend, sat across from his Navajo friend and FBI Agent Raven

Shelly, age 33. The two drank coffee and had split a pie from the evidence of leftover crumbs on the plate. Samuel watched Treehorn enter the establishment, his face stoic. Raven missed Treehorn's entrance due to his anxiety, "I don't know how my badge ended up on a dead woman."

Treehorn shook his head as he approached his friends.

Samuel Bear poked his young FBI friend, "Now is a good time to confess."

"I had nothing to do with that woman. You believe me, right?" wailed Agent Shelly.

Samuel poked again. "I believe you're an incompetent pissant who can't hold onto his badge." He watched as Treehorn held his friend's badge in his hand. "You should be fired."

Treehorn set the badge on the table to put his friend out of his misery. "It was planted."

"My badge! Treehorn!" Several customers glanced at the men as they stood and greeted each other.

The Lakken Energy men recognized Treehorn as a newcomer and as law enforcement. None of them missed the gun and badge attached to his belt, either.

"When Mancuso told me it was your badge on a dead body, I feared the worst," Treehorn stated.

Raven understood the unspoken words. Treehorn cared.

"I feared Mancuso when I couldn't find the badge," Raven countered.

"How did you lose it, pissant? That's an official inquest," Treehorn grilled Raven.

"Honestly, I have no clue. I had it with me when I ate here, then I drove to the FBI housing. I backtracked: diner, drive, and housing. It just disappeared."

"If you didn't misplace it, then someone intentionally lifted it from you, but why?"

"I don't know," Raven muttered. "It made no sense to lift my badge and plant it on a dead body a few hours later."

"It makes perfect sense. Someone doesn't trust you or the local FBI. They wanted me here. It catches Washington's attention really quick when an FBI badge is found on a murder victim. Oh, and Mancuso wants you to call him," Treehorn asked, "Did you know Darcy Clearwater?"

Raven shook his head. "No. We've only been here two days for our own case."

Treehorn added, "She was from the Tábąąhá Clan east of Page. She graduated from the University of Arizona with a geology degree," Treehorn looked at Samuel. "Did you or Tribal know her?"

Samuel Bear shook his head, "No. There's no record or any history with the NNP."

Raven continued, "The coroner asked us about the note."

"I didn't know her, and I have no clue why she wanted me called," Treehorn stated.

"Did Dr. Reynolds have any new information on my case?" Raven asked.

"Just preliminary tests, but she believes the dresses connect our cases," Treehorn whispered.

"The doctor is smart and cute," Samuel watched as Treehorn's face flushed.

"She wears a ring." Treehorn never missed a detail.

"You noticed?" Raven poked his friend.

"Someone said she's single," Samuel tag-teamed.

"Can we focus on the case?" Treehorn snapped.

"You've been alone too long," Samuel stated on a somber note. "Skyler would want you to find happiness during your time here."

Treehorn ignored them as the waitress approached. "Just water please." She nodded and returned to the kitchen.

He glanced at the customers. Their work clothes and attitude separated them.

"You have a missing person; I have a dead geologist employed by Lakken Energy." Treehorn refocused them to the crimes.

"You believe there's a connection?" Raven asked.

"He doesn't believe in coincidences." Samuel nodded toward Treehorn. It was a long-standing belief.

The waitress delivered Treehorn's water. "Are you sure I can't get you some pie or cookies with that? The diner's famous for them."

"Thanks, but I'll pass."

The waitress smiled at him and inched closer. "Patty's the name. You new in town?"

"Thanks for the water. I don't need anything else." Then, the agent ignored her.

Raven and Samuel watched as the waitress hit a dead-end with their friend while he acted like his usual widowed self. The red-faced woman walked away as the two friends shook their heads.

"Tell me about your missing person," Treehorn requested. "I read your report on the plane."

Samuel began the story of Sandy Begay, "It started with the Navajo Nation Police. We got a report from her parents she was missing from Farmington. I sent two officers out and their investigation tracked her here to Williston. "She had a long rap sheet for solicitation in Shiprock, Denver, and Cheyenne."

Raven continued, "She moved to her cousin's, Kaya Massey, here in Williston to work the sex trade with the oil men. Sandy arrived here two weeks ago. Her cousin reported she was here a week, went out soliciting one night, and never returned. Her cousin works for a local house cleaning service and requested updates. She believes someone is holding Sandy against her will. It's a frequent behavior with the wildcatters, catch and release, but it's not very common to be missing so many days. Kaya fears the worst has occurred and Sandy's become another statistic for the Missing and Murdered Indigenous Women."

Samuel added, "Sandy's family in New Mexico hasn't heard from her since she went missing."

Raven continued, "The local state troopers found her purse, with her phone and money inside, on the street. They concluded it was foul play. Her family notified the local FBI. They knew Samuel and I worked the case from the Rez, so they assigned the case to me."

Samuel said, "I volunteered to assist in the investigation. Since the FBI is too busy dealing with frackers, they wouldn't focus on a missing Dine."

Treehorn focused on facts, "Any new leads since you arrived?"

Raven shook his head, "That's the problem. There isn't a single lead. She just disappeared. No one saw anything."

"Tell me about Williston," Treehorn said.

Raven started. "This oil-and-gas boomtown is eighteen years old. The local FBI field office is run by Louise Buckman. The crime rates have tripled compared to other areas. A sense of lawlessness prevails. The townspeople feel like they're living in a western town where money buys a level of protection from the law."

"I spoke with the state troopers. The prostitution here is a revolving door. The girls are banged up terribly with beatings and assaults. When they're not on their backs, they're mules for the drug trade," Samuel said.

Raven addressed the larger issue, "The FBI and DEA are busy twenty-four seven monitoring major crimes while the lesser crimes go unpunished. Buckman assigned the women's cases to my department because she doesn't want two more unsolved federal cases affecting her field office statistics."

"It doesn't matter what a bean counter determined. What's apparent is that money and crime go hand in hand here," Treehorn commented as he eyed the customers and watched the wildcatters abuse the diner staff. They slapped the waitresses on their bottoms and accosted them with inappropriate caresses and hugs. No one opposed the behavior that appeared to be a norm. "Is this how Lakken workers treat people?" Treehorn looked at Samuel who nodded.

One brawny oil worker removed the wallet from his pocket and cash fell to the floor.

The agent watched as a young Lakota boy dropped his towel over the money as he refilled coffee cups. He scooped up the towel and money in a slick shenanigan. Treehorn met the kid's eyes. He opened his jacket which showed the kid his gun and badge.

A white man, sitting in the corner booth, observed the agent's action, then the boy's reaction.

The kid's shoulders sagged. He approached the wildcatter who dropped the money and offered it back to him.

The worker refused the cash, "You keep it, kid. Buy yourself some cookies."

The boy gave Treehorn a look that said, "See!"

The agent watched as the kid returned the coffee pot, went to the rack of cookies, and snagged one.

His mother slapped him with a wooden spoon, "Paco! You eat too many of them and they'll rot your teeth."

The boy smiled and showed his perfect teeth. He looked directly at Treehorn, patted his pocket, and stuck his tongue out at him.

Treehorn cracked a smile as the little con artist escaped out the back door with his haul. His attention returned to the Lakken workers and their ongoing abuse. The smile drained away from his face. He stood, removed his jacket and placed it on the back of the chair. His gun and badge were now on full display for all to see, but it didn't deter the rowdy group as one of them, again, slapped the waitress's behind.

Two well-dressed, elderly Native Americans, in black, red, and white, nodded to the lone white man in the corner booth. He nodded back. The two elders approached the wildcatters and one spoke with a heavy Indian accent, "Do you realize the damage you're doing here?"

One of them stood up and shoved a wad of cash into the Indian's shirt pocket. "That should make you look the other way, Injun man." The Lakken men laughed with arrogance.

The elder removed the money and tossed it on their table with disgust, "No amount of money will fix the destruction you've brought to this land."

One of the frackers replied, "Yes, but it sure makes everyone here richer." The men roared with laughter as the two Indians walked away.

Treehorn watched as the white man, who sat alone and silent in the corner, stood and said something short and clipped to the wildcatters. Whatever was spoken snapped them to attention and they quieted. As he passed Treehorn, the man nodded at him.

Raven watched the man depart, "That's Robert Beltram II, the son of the Lakken Energy CEO."

A wildcatter cat-called him, "What a pussy. He's half the man his father is." The other men voiced their similar opinions with a gang mentality, "That's why they call him *Junior.*" A round of laughter ensued, "Or *By-the-Book Bob.*' another laughed. "He's got the regulation book shoved up his ass." Another asked, "Hey, did you hear that Indian geologist chick turned up dead?"

The enlightening conversation at hand stopped Treehorn from seeking out the younger Beltram. He raised his finger to Samuel and Raven to prevent their interruption as he eavesdropped on the conversation.

"I saw her on Granite Ridge taking samples. I would have liked to have those long legs wrapped around me."

"She was close to Junior. Wonder if he tapped that?"

"Rich and lucky!" They laughed and dumped more cash on their table before leaving the diner.

Treehorn felt the calm that spread over the establishment immediately upon their departure.

The Indian proprietor approached with a decaf coffee pot, "Hi, I'm Cookie Lighthouse. Welcome to Williston."

"John Treehorn, FBI. These are Agent Shelly and Chief Bear of the Navajo Nation Police." Samuel and Raven nodded in greeting.

"Yes, they've been keeping me busy by sharing a homemade pie each evening."

Raven and Samuel laughed, "Guilty as charged."

Treehorn pointed to the large, empty wildcatters' table, "Is that what you and your staff have to deal with daily?"

41

"That bunch? That was the B-team, you want to meet a bunch of a-holes; you should meet the A-team. Brody Hauler runs that miserable bunch. Everyone around here calls him *Body Hauler*. He sends a lot of men to the hospital. He's the meanest SOB, and if you're here long enough, you'll run across him. I wouldn't put it past him to be involved somehow with the abused women here. His goal is keeping the men happy. In return, they work hard to make the company money. How much money does one need for happiness?" Cookie shook her head.

"I'm investigating the death of Darcy Clearwater. She was the Lakken Energy geologist they were talking about."

"Oh, Darcy. She was very nice. She was in here a lot with Bobby Junior. They always had work spread out on their table." The proprietor thought for a few seconds. "She was kind to my boy." She glanced behind her, "Where's that cookie bandit? Kids, they eat and run."

"Can you contact us if you hear anything?" Treehorn asked as he handed her his card.

"Oh, you should talk to Jasper Redmond. He's a retired FBI agent. He works at the MMIW, you know, the Missing and Murdered Indigenous Women's movement. Two of their members just left. They have an office up at the community center. She volunteered up there, helping abused women in the area. I'm glad you're here. Those bozos"—points to where the B-team guys were sitting—"take too much of the local police's time with their DUIs, the prostitution, and there was even a kidnapping last month." She paused to take a breath. "Lucky for her, she was returned to her family a couple days later. An abusive boyfriend was holding her against her will. Stuff like that puts us all on edge. This was a wonderful town, a community, before the energy company came to town. Greed and money destroyed everything that was important here. My husband works the fields. We're saving money so we can sell and return to our Cheyenne River Lakota Nation."

Treehorn nodded, "Agent Shelly is investigating a missing Navajo woman, Sandy Begay. I see you have her poster pinned to your bulletin board."

"That one is another sad and lost cause. Here one day and gone the next. She'll be just another red dress hung by the MMIW," Cookie added. "Do you guys need anything else?"

"No, I'll pay for their order." Treehorn pointed to his friends.

She smiled, "On the house, boys. And, I'll keep my ears open." Cookie accepted the agent's business card. "I'll tell my girls, too."

"Thank you." Treehorn finished his water while the others finished their drinks in silence.

Samuel addressed a somber event, "The coroner should be releasing Darcy's body tomorrow. I'll accompany her home to the reservation."

Treehorn and Raven nodded in solemn respect. "Her family would appreciate that."

"There's no reason for me to stay here with you on the case," Samuel noted. "What about the pissant here?" Samuel nodded toward their friend.

"Hey!" Raven uttered, "I'm getting sick of that."

"Then, stop acting like one!" Samuel added.

Treehorn smiled. "Mancuso said it's my call. He'll stay a few days to work here with me. I don't believe in coincidences. We have two Navajo women—one dead, one missing—in the same boomtown. Something's happening here. Tomorrow I'll set up at the field office, then Raven and I will examine Darcy's apartment after CSU finishes with it. After that, we'll pay Lakken Energy and the MMIW office a visit to find out if either of them can speculate on a motive for murder."

Raven added, "We should have the DNA results back from the lab to verify if the red dress belonged to Sandy. We shouldn't release that information."

"I agree," Treehorn added. "The killer made a mistake."

"We don't know if Sandy is dead or just a missing Navajo at this point," Raven added. "I'm praying for her safe return."

"I think we're past that, Raven. The only way a woman would be caught dead wearing another woman's dirty dress is if a serial killer accidentally redressed her in it."

Raven and Samuel wanted to disagree with their friend and FBI agent, but as trained law enforcement officers, they knew from experience that Treehorn possessed a brilliant investigative mind and rarely misjudged a situation. If by chance he had, it was quickly corrected.

"Have a nice trip home, Samuel. You're lucky, you get to go home to your wife," Raven uttered.

Samuel gave Raven a swift kick on the shin.

"I'm sorry." Raven realized the mistake. His friend would never see his wife again.

Treehorn let Raven's statement slide while he examined the police photo of Sandy Begay, the twenty-six-year-old, black-haired, brown-eyed Navajo, on his phone, "Let's find her so we can return her to her family."

Someone's shallow breathing echoed in the darkened windowless room. Heavy footsteps approached, and the panicked breathing increased. A key released the lock's tumblers which caused a whimpering sound to emanate from the corner, a sound akin to a wounded trapped animal. The single door opened and the lamp from the hallway cast a patch of light bright enough to show a threadbare blanket which provided inadequate coverage for the woman's bruised and naked back. The chains from shackled wrists rattled against the stone wall as the woman tried to evade her captor. A grimy, oil-covered man placed a compact leather whip and condom on a table.

The sound of his zipper interrupted her whimpering.

He whispered, "Mommy!"

The woman raised her gray-haired head as she whimpered. Strands of black hair poked out from beneath the short, curly wig that framed the face of Raven's missing Navajo, Sandy Begay.

The male hand raised the whip over the woman's terror-filled face as her screams reverberated in the small prison, "It's time for you to pay."

46

Chapter Four

FBI Office, Williston, North Dakota

Treehorn telephoned his supervisor to update him on the status of the investigation.

"Leo Mancuso."

"Treehorn here."

"I read your email and the coroner's preliminary report. You have one week to deal with your murder victim and turn it over to the locals."

"Yes, sir."

"Since Agent Shelly's missing person is still missing, you have him until week's end. Work the two cases."

"Yes."

"How did Agent Shelly misplace his badge?"

"I believe someone intentionally lifted it and placed it on the body to get the Feds' attention. Someone didn't trust the local FBI. The evidence appears to link Shelly's and my cases. I think there's more here than a simple murder."

"What are you saying?"

"The preliminary results will be back today, and they can shed some light, but I think we have a serial killer here."

"Don't put that in any report until you have proof!" Mancuso ordered.

"Understood."

"Tell Shelly he's not off the hook with his misplaced badge."

"I will."

"Buckman heads up the Williston, ND office. The director assigned a woman to deal with the significant crimes against women in the area."

"I'll update her, today."

"Keep me posted."

"Yes, sir."

Treehorn and Raven started work at the FBI office before operating hours but from the activity in the booking room, it appeared to be a twenty-four seven operation. The field office was an old converted hotel with the majority of the offices keeping their bathrooms. The courtyard was converted into glass conference and meeting rooms, creating an open, airy feeling. Their office location appeared to be the farthest from the local agents who resented their presence. Treehorn and Raven thought this point of view was ridiculous, considering there was enough crime to go around and they supposedly were all on the same team.

Raven examined Sandy Begay's missing person report while Treehorn organized Darcy Clearwater's information for the bulletin board.

Agent Donovan stopped at the doorway and tossed a fake badge on Raven's desk, "Just in case you misplace yours, again."

Raven stayed silent, but Treehorn watched his friend's face redden.

"Donovan, where are the sexual harassment complaint forms?" Treehorn demanded.

Donovan's face flushed red, too, as he turned and scurried away like a rat. He remained silent as he passed his supervisor in the hallway.

FBI supervisor, Louise Buckman, was fifty-five. She was a single woman, married to her job, who volunteered for this isolated field office position. The FBI wanted a woman to address the disproportional female to male ratio of victims and her numbers showed she had made some headway.

The agent sensed her before she arrived at the door, "Treehorn?"

"Yes," he acknowledged.

"My office." She didn't wait for his response. She heard the snickers and comments from her agents. They didn't like the agents on temporary assignment. Buckman stared at her crew, and the office went silent. She didn't take kindly to her agents' lack of professionalism or their treatment of fellow agents.

Treehorn arrived at her glass-enclosed office without a side glance.

"Close the door."

Buckman had two chairs in front of her desk. He took neither but stood at attention. No, she reassessed her opinion. That was his natural posture. He wasn't cut from the same cloth as the other FBI agents. She wouldn't have guessed that he was half Navajo Indian except for the eyes, brown on the outside, blue on the inside. Merit awards, commendations, dedicated, and widowed. Loved and lost. She observed he still wore his wedding ring. Buckman realized as she assessed him, that he assessed her.

Her hair was professionally dyed close to her natural color, manicured nails, no rings, minimal makeup, pantsuit, a size ten. She wore the posture of a dedicated, no-nonsense supervisor well. Treehorn watched as she glanced at her staff and how they complied with her non-verbal command. They respected her.

"Louise Buckman." She held her hand out.

"John Treehorn." Her handshake was as strong as her demeanor.

"Settling in?"

Treehorn nodded once.

"I apologize that it's not the Ritz. This structure was part of the Lewis and Clark Trail. As for an FBI field office, the smart agents don't stay here long. They put in their minimum required time, and then transfer out. I guess they think crime and justice are different in better locations. Mancuso told me to cooperate one hundred percent with you. I had my reservations about having you here, but he assured me that even if this person was your wife"— Buckman placed that dig at Treehorn and he didn't move a hair— "you'd fulfill your duties. He said if I had a problem with that, he'd have the director call me. So, what makes you so special?"

"I do the job and I don't stop until justice is served. I've visited the body dump location, the morgue, and conferred with Agent Shelly."

Buckman held up her hand. "I don't micromanage. If there's something you feel I need to know, tell me. Don't waste my time. I know you'll do your job. Fair enough? What questions do you have?"

"What can you tell me about Lakken Energy and the crime here?"

Buckman pursed her lips and gave Treehorn a serious fixed stare. "Number one problem. Lakken Energy, boomtown, employs ninety-five percent of the population directly and indirectly. The crime increased in direct relation to the cash influx. I've lost count of the years they've been here, but every year it's been hell for this town. We have all the major crimes represented: murders, manslaughters, rapes, aggravated assaults, and robberies. The largest percentage of crimes here are against women. When it's not the women, it's the drugs. The DEA set up a field office here and dealt with products coming into the area from Canada and across state lines." She glanced out her window at the town. "The townspeople didn't envision this disaster when the energy company arrived. They wanted the money and refused to consider any repercussions. Now, they demand for us to 'fix' it."

Treehorn offered his observation, "You have Lakken Energy workers and crime on one side, the FBI and law enforcement on the other, and the townspeople in the middle forced to swallow the bitter pill of progress to survive and make a living here."

"That sums it up. Now, for the issues at hand: we could have dealt with Shelly's badge issue."

"I believe someone lifted his badge and planted it intentionally on the dead body. They wanted the FBI's attention, not the locals. I'm here now. Mancuso will address Agent Shelly."

"Fair enough. Did you know the victim, Darcy Clearwater?"

"No."

"Do you have any idea why she asked for you?"

"No clue. The fingerprints prove that someone went to great lengths to plant the note on the body to get me here. She got her last wish."

"A note and a badge on a body, do you know what that tells me? She may not have known you personally, but she needed your help. Something else is going on and I know you'll dig until you discover it. It's the reason she's dead. The person who planted the note and badge may know the killer and the reason for the killing."

Agent Treehorn agreed, "And, their life's now in danger."

Buckman nodded. "What's the COD?"

"Blunt force trauma. Sexual contact prior to and post-mortem."

Buckman pursed her lips again as Treehorn recited the results, knowing it had serious ramifications. The area was a cesspool of deviant behavior. "Your victim worked for Lakken and is Indian. The tensions here run high between the workers and the Natives. I want this case cleared off my desk ASAP to prevent any additional problems."

Treehorn nodded once.

"Did you see the red dresses hung around the area? They represent the Missing and Murdered Indigenous women. Is Darcy another red dress?"

"She was murdered," Treehorn answered candidly, "and she found a way to get me a message. I believe she tried to tell me there was a crime here, and I believe that it's the motive for her death."

"Interview Jasper Redmond, he's a retired Fed who donates his time up at the Missing and Murdered Indigenous movement. He may have some insight into your victim and Shelly's."

Buckman's computer dinged. She read from the document that appeared on her computer screen, "DNA results from your victim's dress came back. It matches

Agent Shelly's missing woman, Sandy Begay. Your two cases are now officially connected." Buckman clicked on her screen and the document printed. "Find Sandy Begay, Agent Treehorn. Under no circumstances am I to hear 'serial killer', do you understand?"

Treehorn nodded once.

She glanced out her office window and observed many of her agents watching Treehorn. He either didn't notice or didn't care.

Buckman searched the staff and located Agent Donovan, "You've been here less than twenty-four hours and I see you already found the squeaky wheel of Agent Dennis Donovan."

"He was harassing Dr. Reynolds."

"I assign him to non-women cases. What does that tell you? Did you witness the harassment?"

"Yes," Treehorn answered, "but the ME refused to report it."

"Write it up. Place it in a blank envelope on my desk. I'll decide what to do with him. Agent Donovan is good when he's on his game, but pretty much a misogynistic asshole any other time. I keep him on a short leash. He's assigned to the DEA task force. Drug runners are busy across Idaho and the Canadian border. It's a violent division for agents in this area."

Treehorn understood the unspoken words. It's one way to get rid of an unwanted agent. He wouldn't underestimate this FBI supervisor.

"We no longer need the Navajo Nation Police here since your arrival."

"Chief Bear is accompanying the body back to the reservation when the coroner releases it."

Buckman nodded, "If Agent Shelly or you need anything, just ask."

"Yes, ma'am."

"Tell Agent Shelly not to misplace his badge again while he's in my jurisdiction. Stay away from my agents if you can. If you have any trouble with them, you deal with it. They may not like you being here, in their territory, but they know I won't tolerate any disrespect."

Buckman pointed to the door, and Treehorn nodded, understanding his exit cue.

He returned to the conference room and handed Raven the lab results. "The DNA from the dress is Sandy Begay's. The results connect our cases."

"Oh, man," Raven prayed. "I hope she's still alive,"

"I agree, and I don't want another body turning up with my name on it."

"I pulled information on both women." Raven pointed to the bulletin board.

Treehorn examined it. "Let's assume this board is neither secure nor confidential. Let's keep it posted with only available law enforcement data." Both agents watched as Agent Donovan slithered around the staff area. "We'll secure all other information we wish to keep private as a precaution."

It didn't take long for the bulletin board to become covered with background information from the two cases, including a map of Williston, North Dakota with a smaller image of the Navajo Indian Reservation.

Raven pinned the two women's Arizona and New Mexico driver's license enlargements to the board with their labels.

Darcy Clearwater, Navajo, age thirty-two, University of Arizona graduate. Geologist, Lakken Energy. Single. COD: Blunt force trauma.

Sandy Begay, Navajo, age twenty-six. High school: Farmington. Prostitute. Single. Status: Missing.

"They lived in different areas of the reservation. One was educated and the other had a criminal history of prostitution, criminal mischief, and drug offenses."

"Darcy worked here for over two years. Sandy arrived in Williston two weeks ago."

Two red dress images were attached to the board. One was labeled Sandy Begay. The other was from a dress shop and labeled Darcy Clearwater.

"We didn't know either of these women personally. Let's check the database to see if either have a history with the FBI," Treehorn stated.

"I'll research other federal agencies, too," Raven added.

Treehorn focused on the board. "Darcy lived near Page. We both graduated from the University of Arizona, but we didn't attend during the same time frame. The two women had Navajo in common."

Raven added, "Sandy attended high school in Farmington. She's been arrested in Arizona, New Mexico, Colorado, Wyoming, and North Dakota, every time for solicitation. Williston was the first area where it appeared she came into contact with Darcy Clearwater and/or Lakken Energy."

"Why did you list Lakken Energy?" Treehorn asked.

"Lakken Energy employees were Sandy's only clients."

Treehorn nodded in agreement. "Pull their employee records. Start with violent felons first, sexual abusers, and domestic violence cases. Flag the ones that have juvenile records, even if they're sealed."

"She was here for seven days and, now, she's been missing for seven. We need to re-interview her family and find out if Darcy and Sandy were in contact with each other."

The senior Fed's phone rang, "Agent Treehorn."

"Sir, this is CSU Amanda Wilkerson. We've finished up at the victim's apartment. Do you want a verbal report, or would you like to come here for a walk through? We have confirmed this as the murder location."

"We'll meet you there," Treehorn told her. He definitely wanted a visual on the crime scene.

Darcy Clearwater's Apartment

Treehorn drove to Darcy's apartment and Raven accompanied him, in case there was anything there that connected their cases. A hat-wearing, military veteran guarded the apartment, sworn in by the local sheriff's department for the purpose of conducting non-combative assignments. Treehorn presented his identification, "FBI, Special Agents Treehorn and Shelly."

"Nice to meet you. Sign in please." The guard handed the agent a clipboard. As Treehorn printed and signed his name, he noted that Dr. Reynolds had arrived and left. He passed the document to Raven.

"All the able-bodied deputies are busy arresting oil workers who are up to no good."

"You're doing a much-appreciated service here."

The man grunted. Treehorn offered his hand to the veteran who shook it, "Thank you for your service to our country."

Raven followed suit, "Thank you."

Treehorn knocked and opened the door. The one-bedroom apartment appeared neat but was now covered in crime scene paraphernalia.

A CSU tech waited for the men, then acknowledged the agents. "I'm Amanda Wilkerson."

"Treehorn and Shelly."

"Come on in." The tech handed the agents shoe covers and latex gloves. "We finished collecting all the evidence, but put these on as a precaution, in case we need to come back." Yellow numbered triangles covered the apartment. Wilkerson handed Treehorn a tablet loaded with crime scene images.

"Where was she killed?" Treehorn examined the layout.

Wilkerson pointed, "Here, next to her desk. It appeared she fell on the trash can, probably from a blow delivered by the killer. We recovered blood. As she lay dying, someone stomped on her wrist, here. We recovered tiny shards of broken glass from the watch crystal." The area of carpet was cut and removed by the technicians and the metal wastebasket was bagged.

"Walk me through it." Treehorn flicked through the images on the tablet.

"Her laptop and phone are missing, no other signs of robbery. There was over four-hundred dollars in cash, untouched, in the desk."

Treehorn advanced the images on the tablet. On the corner of her desk sat a glass award and next to that, written achievements. He examined the images cataloged.

"We bagged work clothes, boots, and her engineer clothing. We'll test everything."

"Did she reside somewhere else? This place doesn't look lived in," Treehorn observed.

"We agree. In the bathroom, there were two toothbrushes, one blue, one pink, men's and women's deodorants, and men's clothing in the dryer. We packaged everything, but it feels like a transitory motel."

"What else?"

"We removed hair samples from the shower. The toilet seat was left up and we recovered a thumbprint on the lever." Wilkerson pointed to the rear door, "It was unlocked, and we recovered more prints from it." The tech walked to an adjoining area and pointed to the yellow markers, "In the living room, we recovered a glass of water, and in the bedroom, a milk glass with a snack on the nightstand. We fingerprinted both and sent them for DNA testing."

Treehorn examined the inside of the closet. Two black business dresses and one man's suit, with a dress shirt, hung on the rod in dry-cleaning plastic. "Do we have the man's identification?"

"Not yet."

Treehorn examined the bedroom. A Frank Howell lithograph hung on one wall. Two professional pottery pieces sat on the dresser, but it was the basket hanging on the wall that caught the Navajo agent's attention.

They returned to the desk area where an answering machine sat. "Any messages?"

"One from the local pharmacy. It's logged, so just hit play to hear it."

Raven pushed the button: *"This is Williston Pharmacy. Your prescription is ready for pickup."*

Treehorn guided Raven's eyes to the document above Darcy Clearwater's desk with a discreet nod. Pinned to the wall was the front-page main story from the *Indian Times* newspaper. The headline: *"FBI and Navajo Nation Police Solve Cold Case Murder"* was illuminating. The newspaper image showed John Treehorn and Raven Shelly wearing their FBI badges, and Samuel Bear in his Navajo Nation Police uniform.

Raven pointed CSU Wilkerson to the article. "Bag it and tag it."

Treehorn watched the technician as she placed it into an evidence bag. "It may explain how she knew I was FBI, but not why I was called."

"We'll send a report to you and the coroner as soon as we have them prepared, and we'll secure the apartment until further notice."

"Thanks," Treehorn glanced around the apartment one last time.

"Samuel's at the Painted Pony," Raven offered. "Do you want to swing by and grab a coffee before we visit Lakken?"

"Sounds like a plan."

Chapter Five

Dr. Samantha Reynolds opened the door of the Painted Pony Diner in need of a large coffee. An early morning, death by natural causes had pulled her from her comfortable bed. She found Police Chief Samuel Bear eating his brunch. "Good morning, Chief Bear."

"Good morning, Dr. Reynolds. Join me?"

"Thanks." Samantha examined the face of the police chief. His long black hair was lined with silver strands while his black eyes focused on her tired eyes.

"Out early this morning?"

"DOA, elderly man, natural causes. Funny thing, his wife died a week ago from natural causes, too. His family thinks he died from a broken heart."

"I believe that's possible," he sympathized.

The coroner hesitated, "I should have test results back later today on Darcy Clearwater's case. I know it's not yours."

Samuel Bear waited for her inquiry about his friend. He wasn't disappointed.

"Tell me about John Treehorn."

"He's a good man. One of the bravest, most dedicated, smartest investigators I know. I've watched him grown since his birth."

"Tell me about his wife." Samantha felt an invisible wall rise.

Samuel's reserved voice continued, "Skyler? Kind, smart, beautiful, she could make Treehorn laugh with just a smile." The memory soothed Samuel's weary soul. "She was my niece."

"Was?"

Samuel's face darkened with sadness, "She died."

"I'm sorry."

"Murdered fifteen years ago. Seems like yesterday."

"That must have been very traumatic."

"Yes, for everyone. Treehorn's gained the ability to move beyond the pain that would have destroyed a lesser man."

"I'm glad he's remarried and moved on."

"Treehorn's single."

"He wears a wedding ring."

"It provides him comfort." Samuel's eyes squinted at the medical examiner and he cocked his head. "Why are you asking questions about a man's marital status when you, yourself, are wearing a bridal set?"

"These were my mother's. She died three years ago."

Samuel gave her the push she needed, "It worked for Treehorn."

"Did he mention me?"

Samuel shook his head. "No, but Treehorn doesn't miss the details."

"Good to know."

"That goes for the job, too. He'll find who's responsible for Darcy's death and he'll hunt them down regardless of how long it takes. He's never forgotten a victim."

"That's an admirable trait," Samuel added as the waitress delivered their coffees.

Treehorn and Raven entered the diner and saw Samuel Bear sitting with the ME.

"Hello," Treehorn greeted them.

A startled Samantha spilled her coffee.

"I'm sorry. I didn't mean to surprise you." Treehorn grabbed up some napkins to help the doctor clean the spill. "Are you burned?"

"No, I'm fine. Thanks."

Samuel and Raven watched the interaction. Samuel moved over and Raven immediately sat down next to him.

Treehorn stared at his two friends as he sat next to the doctor.

The waitress arrived, took their drink order, and left them with a pile of napkins.

Samuel and Raven watched their friend's face flush, an occurrence they'd never witnessed. The pair observed the coroner's face redden, too. They were assholes about it and smiled.

The ME broke the silence, "I'm finished with Darcy Clearwater and the body has been released."

Samuel Bear spoke, "I've been in contact with Darcy's family. I'll take her home to the reservation today. You don't need me here."

"I'll keep you posted if we get any information on Sandy Begay," Raven told Samuel for his records.

"Thanks, that'll provide some comfort to the family," Samuel reflected on their loss.

The ME added, "I should have some lab back by the end of the day. I hope it will shed some light on both cases. I'll fax over the results," Samantha added.

"Thanks," Treehorn nodded.

Samuel nudged Raven, "Let me up. I'm going to call the wife and let her know I'm coming home. You should call your wife, too."

"I'll call Dana, later." Samuel kicked Raven who rubbed his shin as the pair stood up from the booth. "I'll surprise her with a call."

Treehorn shook his head. "I'm sorry about those two."

"They care for you." Samantha smiled.

When the waitress delivered their coffees, Treehorn asked, "Can I add two black coffees, to go, to the order, please?" His sudden eagerness to depart dampened Samantha's spirit.

"Samuel told me you lost your wife. I'm sorry."

Treehorn glanced at his wedding band, "It was a long time ago." He glanced at her rings. "Why do you wear a wedding set if you're single?"

"They're my mother's," Samantha hesitated and touched them, "I wear them to keep assholes like Donovan away."

"Has it worked?" Treehorn asked the rhetorical question.

Samantha laughed, "No. Nothing stops men like him." She yawned. "I'm sorry. I was out early this morning with an elderly death."

Treehorn contemplated asking Samantha out for dinner but the waitress interrupted as she delivered his order, then Samuel and Raven returned. He ground his teeth.

"We're interviewing Lakken Energy and Jasper Redmond of the MMIW movement today to see if either can provide a motive for Darcy's death. She had a recent edition of the *Indian Times* on her bulletin board." Treehorn showed her the image of the front page on his phone. "It may explain how she knew my name, but not why she wanted me called."

Samuel responded, "You're here and you'll find the answers."

Treehorn stood and shook Samuel's hand. "Have a safe trip home, my friend."

Raven shook Samuel's hand, too. "I'll keep you posted with any updates on both cases."

"Be safe and watch each other's back," Samuel added.

Treehorn informed Samantha. "We'll keep you posted, too."

Samuel and Raven glanced at Treehorn. He never shared his investigations.

"Thanks. I hope to see you later," Samantha smiled.

The Lakken Energy offices were located outside of town, off the main highway, where the sprawling yard and storage buildings could contain the millions of dollars in equipment required for the oil and gas exploration giant. Enormous trucks, cranes, and pipe filled the compound which was surrounded by a tall, chain link fence.

Robert Beltram and his son Bobby watched from the second floor, office window as the recognizable law enforcement vehicle stopped at the main entrance gate. The younger man looked at his namesake, "You own this," and walked out of his father's office.

The first thing Treehorn and Raven noticed as they approached the compound was the North Dakota State Police vehicle with its red and blue caution lights flashing. Treehorn eased his vehicle past the trooper who nonchalantly leaned against a barricade. It was one of the several barricades erected to prevent a group of sign-holding protesters from entering the compound. It also served to keep all parties safe and out of harm's way from large vehicles and traffic. The protesters were of various ages and ethnicities, carrying signs that read: *STOP ABUSING OUR WOMEN!*, *WE ONLY HAVE ONE EARTH!*, and *STOP THE GREED!*

Treehorn braked at the security guard house before its tire-spike entrance and presented his identification, "FBI

Special Agents John Treehorn and Raven Shelly. Here to see Robert Beltram."

The low-level cop wannabe named Jimi Veluta examined his clipboard. "You don't have an appointment."

"We don't need one."

The guard didn't lower the tire spikes; instead, he picked up a telephone and called his superior.

Treehorn and Raven watched the protesters in their mirrors. The younger agent voiced what his co-worker thought, "I admire their protests, but nothing stops the destruction of Mother Earth when there's money to be made."

Treehorn added, "When the last tree is cut, and the last stream is polluted, man will realize he can't eat money."

The guard pointed to an office building, "Mr. Beltram's office entrance is there and you can park in front." The guard pushed a button and the spikes grated as they lowered into the metal.

Treehorn and Raven walked into the lobby and were promptly stopped by an administrator named Delores as she guarded the elevators, "No weapons are allowed upstairs. Please place them in the security lockers for your convenience."

Treehorn scowled at the woman. "We're FBI and we're not surrendering our side arms."

The administrator's smile didn't reach her eyes. "Then, you're not meeting with Mr. Beltram, today."

"He knows we're here?" Agent Treehorn countered.

The woman uttered, "Maybe."

"Then, *maybe* we'll wait for him." Treehorn and Raven removed their coats and hung them on the rack provided. They folded their arms and didn't budge.

Treehorn spoke Navajo to Raven, "Do you want to make a bet, my friend?"

Raven answered in their first language, "No, I always lose to you."

"She's deciding whether to call her boss or suffer his wrath when he's made to wait."

"She has backbone; she'll wait for his call. Beltram will credit her for doing her job."

The administrator spoke, "You know, it's rude to speak in a foreign language while others are present."

Treehorn curled his lip in contempt and sarcastically replied, "Learn Navajo, then you'll understand."

The ringing of the telephone prevented her response, "They're in the lobby and they're refusing to stow their weapons." She listened. "Yes, sir." The woman looked at

Raven and ignored Treehorn, "You may go up." She pushed a button on her desk and the elevator doors opened.

Raven, being a pissant, asked the woman, "Is Agent Treehorn allowed, too?"

The woman answered by turning her back to both men.

"You should have bet, you would've won," Treehorn added in Navajo loud enough so Delores heard. The elevator doors closed and rose. "Weapons secured? Does he feel threatened?"

"The protesters outside?" Raven asked his fellow agent.

"When you return to the office, research Lakken's history and see what threats have been filed by them or against them with the agencies."

"You think Lakken could have been the target since Darcy was their employee?"

"The truth always spills out. It just takes time."

Ruth Rogers, a middle-aged brunette, waited for the men as they stepped out of the elevator, "Please follow me, gentlemen."

Treehorn and Raven accompanied her down a thick, carpeted hallway. They passed a glass-lined conference

room and several offices. The nameplates read Mark
Garland, Attorney; Robert Beltram II, Operations; and
Darcy Clearwater, Geology & Engineering. A large, glass
artwork bubbled as the water flowed from it. It lined the
entire hallway along the conference room and ended at the
CEO's office door.

Robert Beltram's office showed the epitome of a
successful businessman. A wall of windows overlooked his
operation. The specialized glass and sound-proofed room
provided a barrier between the working man and his
administration. Oak-paneled walls were covered with
images of Lakken Energy operations and awards.
Photographs with senators, judges, and dignitaries lined
another wall. A heavy mahogany desk sat front and center,
bare except for the phone and a single pen. Robert Beltram
walked out of his private bathroom and held out his hand
for introductions, a distinguished man at age sixty who
wore his power well. "Robert Beltram, CEO, Lakken
Energy."

"FBI Special Agents John Treehorn and Raven
Shelly." Treehorn and Raven presented their identification
and shook the hand of the gray-haired man in the bespoke
suit.

Treehorn eyed the other occupant in the room. A dark-haired, fifty-year-old man, expensively dressed, sat in the corner and didn't stand during the introductions.

"My attorney, Mark Garland. He's here to listen to what you have to say. Have a seat. Thank you, Ruth, and please close the door." As soon as Robert heard the *click,* he turned on the FBI agents, "Why are out-of-town FBI agents here investigating a local murder?"

"How did you know we're not local? We don't give out details of our operations." Treehorn shut him down.

Beltram shrugged, walked to his wall of windows and examined his operation. "People hate us for extracting oil and gas from the ground, but all of them uses it to power their cars, heat their homes, and to cook their food. They curse us every day. How do you define irony?" The CEO sat behind his desk and activated a hidden button. The wall of windows changed to a high-tech solid image of a single oil well. "My first million came from that well. I've never forgotten where I come from. The money I make made me the man I am today, and I continue to build it, for my son."

Treehorn let Beltram feed his ego, the story of the rich white man; Treehorn had heard it all before. "Darcy Clearwater."

"Yes, of course. Darcy was a valuable asset to our team. I've offered a $500,000 reward for information leading to the arrest and prosecution of her killer."

"What was her job?"

"Head engineer and geologist, and to put it in terms you'll understand: she found the oil and gas under the ground so that we could extract it." Robert opened a top drawer in his desk and removed a Cuban cigar, then clipped its end. "Hope you boys don't arrest me for this."

Treehorn declined his bait. "We haven't determined a motive for her death."

"She made me a very rich man, Agent Treehorn, and that, in turn, made my employees very rich. We valued her here."

"What about you? Did you have a reason to murder her?" The agent asked.

"She was an asset, here, and irreplaceable." The CEO took large puffs from his cigar.

"Her laptop and phone are missing. Did she leave either one here?" Treehorn grilled.

"Darcy always had them with her. They were company-issued, encrypted. You'll never see their contents, Mr. Treehorn, when or if they turn up. Lawyers, company secrets, trademarks, you understand right?" The CEO's chest puffed out as he took a big drag off his illegal cigar and gave his lawyer a glance.

The agent wasn't deterred, "Can you tell me what she was working on?"

"She did our environmental studies, which she submitted for approval to Washington. You will have full access to them. My son can provide you with the federal agencies and their contact information."

"Did a company secret get her killed?"

Robert Beltram pressed his intercom button, "Ruth, ask Bobby to come in." He blew smoke rings in the air.

Mark Garland spoke, "When the company-issued items are located, you don't have the right to access them. Do you understand?"

"We will access them with a search warrant, if needed." Treehorn countered.

"Thank you, Agent Treehorn, for showing your intent. The laptop contains proprietary data that we'll block you from accessing, including our intranet."

"Thank you, Mr. Garland, for showing your intent. I'll have a judge's warrant on your desk by the end of the day."

The company lawyer added, "We'll see you at the court hearing."

"It sounds like you're more concerned with your company's secrets than your employee's death. We're here to find a killer."

Bobby Beltram entered the office without knocking which interrupted the conversation. A tanned and athletic thirty-year-old dressed in khakis and dress shirt held out his hand out to the agents. The agents recognized the man from the diner.

"Bobby Beltram."

"FBI Special Agents John Treehorn and Raven Shelly."

Bobby shook their hands. "How can I help?"

"We're trying to establish a motive and timeline for Darcy Clearwater's murder. When was the last time you saw her?"

The CEO answered first, "Monday noon. She left the building to run a study, informed her staff of her time, and she then clocked out at 3 pm. I don't see my employees after work hours. Bobby handles the operations. The state troopers arrived here and notified us of her death."

Treehorn and Raven examined the younger Beltram. They noticed the lines of exhaustion that creased his face and his bloodshot eyes.

"I saw Darcy at 6 pm at the Missing and Murdered Indigenous Women's Movement dinner at the community center. She received the Trident award for her work with the abused women. I left shortly after that. We had a well that blew out, west of Pine Hill pumping station. I was there all night with my men while we extinguished the fire. I received the news of her death when I returned here." Bobby didn't comment on his visit to the morgue.

"How was she killed?" Robert asked.

"Blunt force trauma," Treehorn answered and Bobby's face paled. "Do either of you know if she was working on something here that would provide a motive for her death?"

The CEO replied sharply, "The company wasn't the cause of her death, Agent Treehorn."

"Darcy was a good employee," Bobby said, interrupting his father. "She worked here for over two years. You can verify that her reports which were submitted to the regulatory agencies in Washington were always exemplary."

Treehorn presented a different viewpoint, "I've seen women mistreated in this town. Who had an ax to grind with Darcy as a woman in a senior position?"

Robert Beltram scapegoated the situation, "Agent Treehorn, my men work hard and play harder. That's why we donate money to the local law enforcement agencies. If a crime is committed, the police take care of it."

Bobby added, "Darcy worked effectively with the men, Agent Treehorn. If they didn't play by the rules, they were either transferred to one of our other locations or terminated."

"I'll need a list of those men."

"You'll have the list when I see a warrant, Agent Treehorn. I'm not going to have a witch hunt against my men when you have no proof or motive that any of them was involved in this crime."

Bobby disagreed with his father, "We have nothing to hide. What's wrong with providing a list of the men Darcy had problems with in the past?"

Beltram backed down, "Agent Treehorn, she worked extensively with my son Bobby for the operations. My men knew their place and they knew the consequences of their behaviors."

Bobby added, "She dealt effectively with any problems that arose."

Beltram suggested a motive aside from his company, "You should investigate the Missing and Murdered

Indigenous Movement organization at the community center. She volunteered her time helping the women of that group. One of the men may have taken offense to her sticking her nose in where it didn't belong."

"Jasper Redmond heads the organization, Agent Treehorn. He can tell you who Darcy helped," Bobby added.

"What did she do when she wasn't working or volunteering?" Treehorn continued.

Beltram answered, "I haven't a clue." He reiterated, "I see my employees nine to five. I never talk to them or socialize with them after hours. Bobby deals with everything after 5 pm, unless there's an emergency he can't handle, though that's never occurred. Darcy had a job and she did it." The CEO activated his office window and viewed the protesters outside. "We provide money for living wages, jobs, even health care. It's never enough for some people. The oil was here before they were born, and the oil will be here after they're dead and buried."

Treehorn ignored the attempt at deflection. "Do you know if she was involved with anyone?"

"I have no idea. I don't concern myself with my employees' personal lives. I hire them to work, not fraternize."

Bobby remained silent.

Beltram checked the time on his platinum Rolex. Ruth came into the office and handed her boss a tagged document. "I have a conference call scheduled, gentlemen. Bobby can show you Darcy's office and answer any remaining questions." The CEO signed the document and handed it to Ruth. "Bobby, Darcy's computer and phone are missing. Can you look in her office for them? Secure them when they're found."

Treehorn and Raven stood. "Thank you for your time."

Beltram shook the agents' hands and they followed Bobby out of his father's office.

The administrator stood by the door and waited for the men to leave.

"Please close the door, Ruth."

Treehorn accompanied Bobby Beltram to Darcy's office and they passed his own opened door. Treehorn glanced inside and noticed a bookcase filled with manuals and a modest collection of Native American art.

Bobby entered Darcy's neat office and searched for her computer and phone. "There was a minor earthquake Friday night east of Granite Ridge." Bobby pointed to the area map where twenty red push pins were located. "It's an area that's recently been swarmed with minor quakes. Every time one occurred, Darcy checked the instruments that were positioned there. That was her last duty on Monday afternoon."

"Do you have wells there?"

"Some old, retired wells and some new ones." Bobby showed Treehorn and Raven the maps covering her office wall. They encompassed the complete Lakken Energy projects.

"She was always out in the field and lived out of her Jeep. Well Number 175 blew out here"—Bobby pointed to its location on the map— "and I spent the night putting out its fire. I called her from the well."

"Why did you call her?"

"We're both geologists, Agent Treehorn. I called her to update her on the blowout, but the call went to her voicemail. The state trooper was here when my men and I returned from the well."

Treehorn asked, "Did you leave the well during the night?"

Bobby wasn't offended by the question, "No, Agent Treehorn. It took the whole night for my crew and me to extinguish the fire. We rode there together and returned together. I didn't kill Darcy."

Treehorn examined the map in closer detail and nodded.

"Regardless of what my father says, I can guarantee you'll have the full cooperation of every employee in this investigation, Agent Treehorn. I'll email the list of men to you who had a problem working with her, today."

"What type of personal relationship did you have with her?"

Bobby hesitated, "Are you asking if we were dating? No, Agent Treehorn, we weren't dating. She was my employee."

"Do you know if she was involved with anyone?"

"We talked engineering."

"Do you have any idea why someone would have killed her?"

"No, I don't, Agent Treehorn. A reward has been offered for information. Anything I can do to help, please ask."

"Why did you offer to pay for her funeral?"

Bobby's voice was sad. "She was a valuable member of our team. It was the least I could do with my money."

Treehorn picked up one of Bobby Beltram's business cards. "Can you give me your private cell number, and your father's, in case I need to contact you immediately? I'll need Darcy's for the paperwork." Treehorn watched as he wrote the numbers on the back. The agent handed Bobby one of his cards. "You can send the email to that address. I'm staying at the FBI lodging if you need to contact me after hours."

"Thank you, Agent Treehorn, Agent Shelly. Again, if you have any questions feel free to call me at any time."

The men shook hands and left the younger Beltram staring at the company maps. No receptionist was to be found as the pair left the building. The guard at the main gate lowered the spikes and ignored the men as they departed the grounds.

Treehorn examined the protesters and their prominent signs in more detail as they drove past: *LAKKEN IS KILLING US!*, *WATER IS LIFE!*, and the MMIW sign, *WHERE ARE OUR WOMEN?* Treehorn and Raven acknowledged the state police and wondered what he had failed to do to deserve this detail. As the agents passed the last protester, they heard her plea, "Help us!"

Robert Beltram watched the FBI agents drive past the protesters. He snuffed his cigar out in its ashtray and made a telephone call on his cell. "You have a problem. I was just visited by FBI agents asking questions about Darcy. Get to my office, now." Robert went to his computer and examined the security surveillance images of the FBI agent's visit. He stopped at the image of Treehorn checking in at the main gate with his FBI identification held in his hand. He clicked his keyboard and Treehorn's image and badge enlarged. Robert hit the computer key and his printer came to life.

Beltram's second call was to another person on his payroll. "Donovan? Why didn't you tell me that the FBI was heading Darcy's murder investigation?" The CEO interrupted Donovan's response, "I don't want to hear your sniveling. What do you know?" His face went from a red to a purplish hue as Donovan answered his question. "Keep him busy, so he's not a bother." Beltram smashed his smart phone on his desk and left the staff to clean up his mess.

The same staff avoided Brody Hauler, a mean-spirited man in his early thirties, who came into Robert Beltram's office without knocking. The CEO handed him the image printed from their security cameras of the FBI agent. "Special Agent John Treehorn. I telephoned Donovan. He informed me that someone had placed an FBI badge on Darcy's body."

Brody answered defensively, "So? That has nothing to do with me."

"Why the hell would someone put an FBI badge on a dead body?"

"Is that why you called?" Brody shouted.

"I don't give a shit about Darcy's murder. That's the least of my problems." Robert ordered his top man, who he knew would do anything for him, "I don't want the Feds sniffing around my company. You show his image to every employee. If any of them cooperates with the FBI, they're fired."

Treehorn's vehicle covered miles as he thought of the interview, and he voiced a conclusion to Raven, "Neither Robert or Bobby Beltram murdered Darcy."

"How do you figure?" Raven asked.

"They're both right-handed. Robert signed the document and Bobby wrote on his business card."

"And we know Darcy was killed with a blow from a left-handed man."

"No killer or definitive motive." Treehorn floored the gas pedal and let the horses cover the miles.

Robert pressed a button beneath his desk and a hidden bookcase door opened. He walked through it and approached a single man who sat at a desk covered with computer equipment and hacking devices. The young MIT computer nerd typed on his laptop, which appeared to be connected to all of the other devices.

"Have you accessed it yet?" Robert questioned.

"No," Howie, the computer geek, nervously answered.

"The computer is company's property. I own it - not the dead woman. If you can't hack it, I'll pay someone who can."

"I can hack it. It's just going to take time."

"It's a simple password," Robert argued.

"No, Miss Clearwater installed a complex, password-encryption program. She didn't want anyone accessing this laptop."

"Have you located her phone yet?"

"No," Howie sweated, "It has to be powered on for the GPS to track it. Someone did a battery removal shutdown."

"Can you locate once it's turned on?" Beltram snapped.

"Yes, we can as long as someone is watching for it."
Howie provided a satisfactory answer judging by the look
on Beltram's face.

"Then you better be watching for it twenty-four
seven!" the CEO ordered.

Howie understood the threat.

Chapter Six

Williston Community Center

Treehorn drove to the Williston Community Center, a business that catered to baptisms, weddings, funerals, and housed the offices for the Missing and Murdered Indigenous Women's movement. The community center was a striking architectural landmark made from locally-quarried granite and timbers imported from the Canadian forest. The building sat high on the hillside and overlooked miles of prairie. One would think its strategic location provided shelter and guarded against predators.

The beauty of the stone and timber architecture wasn't lost on Treehorn and Raven as they walked the path towards the entrance of the structure. A large fire roared in a pit. It welcomed all who crossed its threshold. The agents presented their identification to the receptionist, "Special Agents John Treehorn and Raven Shelly to see Jasper Redmond."

"Welcome, gentlemen. I'm Roni Allen. My husband is Trooper Toby Allen. You can hang your coats here." Roni pointed to a closet and the men removed their coats.

"We're examining Darcy's timeline prior to her death and the events that occurred here on Monday night," Treehorn stated.

"Jasper can help you with that. I'll let him know you're here." Roni Allen pointed to a wall behind Treehorn and Raven, "Those are the pictures of the Missing and Murdered Indigenous Women's Movement dinner from Monday evening. Darcy received the Trident Award for Community Service. She's pictured in the center receiving it. I'll let Jasper know you're here."

"Thank you."

The agents examined the photographs. The most prominent image was of Darcy holding a glass trophy with her left hand and wearing her expensive watch. Other photographs showed residents eating and dancing. The last image pictured Bobby Beltram and Darcy conversing with a group of women during pre-dinner drinks. All of the images were time stamped, with this one being 5:50 pm. The CEO's son was in no other images.

Treehorn watched as a distinguished brown-haired, white man approached. If he was surprised at the age of the retired FBI agent, he didn't show it. Jasper Redmond appeared no older than fifty, but he knew he was fifty-five from of his file he had reviewed.

"Special Agents John Treehorn, Raven Shelly."

"Jasper Redmond, retired. Would you gentleman like some refreshments? Cookie Lighthouse dropped off some baked goods this morning."

"I never turn down coffee," Treehorn responded.

"I never turn down anything," Raven added.

The men chuckled.

"No investigator should go hungry or thirsty."

The men settled at the cloth-covered table near the fire with hot coffee and a plate of homemade cookies.

Treehorn knew Jasper Redmond would have already developed his own law enforcement viewpoint in this investigation and hopefully would provide his peers with a needed lead in the search for the killer.

"Darcy Clearwater. I was surprised and saddened to hear of her murder. I've conducted hundreds of investigations, and the people you know hit home the hardest."

"Let's start with... who was Darcy Clearwater?"

"No, Agent Treehorn, let's start first with the Missing and Murdered Indigenous Women's movement. That will tell you who Darcy Clearwater was. The MMIW, as I'm sure you read up on, is a movement out of Canada where indigenous leaders and families have pressured the government to confirm and address the number of missing and murdered indigenous women."

"The FBI has received updates from the RCMP," Treehorn replied.

"The United States has done little to address the issue." Redmond stated. "Did you read the Violence Against Women Act's national study? They found that homicide was the third leading cause of death among Native females, and 75% were killed by either family members or by people they knew. As you're well aware, on some of the US Indian reservations, Native women are murdered at over ten times the national average."

Treehorn and Raven both knew the statistics and saw firsthand the effects in their investigations, month after month, year after year.

"Tribal leaders, law enforcement officers, and prosecutors tell the all-too-familiar story of the violence that goes unaddressed. All we hear of are the tears of pain, loss, and anger that their loved ones are missing or murdered. This is Darcy's story."

"We're listening; go on," Treehorn requested.

"I arrived here a short time before Darcy started her job. It takes no one any length of time to see the violence against the women here. The money changing hands draws them like a magnet and the men feel it gives them the right to prostitute and assault women. Murder is just the end product of the circle of violence. Many of these men were products, themselves, of abusive homes. Adulthood saw no change."

"Where does Darcy fit into this?"

"Darcy was smart. I'm not talking just college-educated smart, but the street smarts of direct, firsthand knowledge of the cycle of abuse. She knew the chain could also be broken."

"What did Darcy do here with the MMIW?" Treehorn pressed.

"She helped women escape from this environment. We have a Circle of Elders who assisted her. They developed a network of locations and people who assisted and relocated the abused women, the women who wanted out but didn't want to return to their abusive homes. They developed an extensive Indian Underground Railroad. The women who wished to be reunited with their families, she made that happen. The women who were brought here against their will, she helped prosecutors make arrests."

"Did her work here get her killed?"

"I don't know. All I know is that she allowed no one to push her around."

"Have you received any information on Sandy Begay's disappearance?" Raven asked.

"No. The MMIW had no contact with Sandy, as we told Buckman when she first inquired and filed the missing person's report."

"Would Darcy have helped Sandy Begay disappear without informing you?" Raven speculated.

"No, we didn't keep secrets. There was no contact with Sandy Begay. I've made inquiries since Buckman's telephone call, but every inquiry became a dead end."

Treehorn asked what Jasper Redmond hadn't elaborated on, "Relocating women is costly. Where does your funding come from to pay for these activities?"

"Darcy donated much of her salary and her stock dividends from her job. We receive donations from families of the missing and the murdered, too."

Treehorn wasn't satisfied with that answer. "That's not enough to cover the operations. Who else donated?"

Jasper hesitated. "Bobby Beltram. He donated a million dollars, anonymously, each year, through Darcy."

"That's commendable. Who knew of their involvement?"

"Nothing stays secret gentlemen, regardless of how hard we've tried."

"Did you receive threats?"

"Yes. The justice system works for the criminal and not for the victims. Moving women isn't a crime but the men who lost their whipping posts didn't take kindly to it. They knew I was a retired Fed. The men could posture all they wanted, but they never attacked us directly. They'd take it out on the women left behind."

"We'll need a list of the men who made threats. Did one of them take it out on Darcy, Monday night? She was murdered after she departed the ceremony."

"The cocktails started at 5:30 pm. We have limited cell service here, but we have a landline for public use. Bobby Beltram received a call regarding a well blowout, and he departed for that emergency around 6 pm. We presented the various awards, with Darcy's being last. The only thing I know is that Darcy received a telephone call here during the banquet and it upset her. No one here can remember who called."

"Can we get photographs of the awards dinner?"

"Roni is copying the images as we speak. We provided cameras with digital cards for the attendees, so everyone could record the event."

"We'll examine all of the images."

"Darcy was very humbled upon receiving her award. She garnered a quiet respect."

"Tell us about the MMIW red dresses," Treehorn requested.

"I'll do you one better, I'll show you."

The agents followed Jasper to a panel. He pressed a button and the floor to ceiling red stage curtains opened. Red dresses covered the whole wall from the floor to the ceiling. A plaque named the exhibit: STOLEN SISTERS. Photographs of Missing and Murdered Indigenous women covered every red dress. Each photograph listed the woman's name and the date of her disappearance. Hundreds of women's photos lined the wall. It brought home the sobering picture; these were the faces of women who were missing or murdered.

Jasper pointed to the women of all ages, "These are our *Stolen Sisters*. We posted all of them from Canada and the United States. We post them all because thousands of people will never stop seeking justice for them."

"Do you believe the red dresses will bring that?" Treehorn asked.

"Justice comes to all, Agent Treehorn, in one form or another. I believed that when I was an agent, and I believe you and your partner do, too. The families and friends of the victims hang dresses as a daily reminder that their loved ones will never be forgotten. Justice is sought, justice will be found. We hang dresses daily to support that cause. The red dress asks the community, 'Where are our women?' And, it reminds everyone there are killers who walk amongst us."

"The history of violence that perpetuates needs to be stopped," Treehorn stated the obvious.

"That is the main cause. It's a sickness festering in their own family, friends, or in neighborhoods of their own community. It's a vicious circle of alcohol, drugs, abuse, and poverty."

"What about this community?"

"There are no permanent relationships here. Here, the violence is from the energy workers. In other places, the violence against women is perpetrated by their own. They escape from one violent household and arrive at a more violent community. The men show they can't live without sex."

The men relocated from the wall to the sun room.

"Look around, gentlemen. Nothing lasts forever. Our prairie disappears like the women here and it's replaced by greed and the destruction of Mother Earth. One day the oil wells will be removed, and the prairie will return, but the bodies will stay buried."

"That's the law of the criminal and their behavior," Treehorn stated the obvious.

"I'm a realist. The love of money is destroying everything here, and no one has plans to stop it. Law enforcement sees it as an ongoing circle of violence and destruction. The local government sees dollar signs and ignores the foregone consequences. The elders protest Lakken Energy on a regular schedule, not just for Mother Earth, but for the women, too. A wise Indian once said, 'Peasants always bear the consequences of kings.' I remind them and their employees, we're here and we're not going away."

"That sounds personal."

"I know there's a killer here and I will not stop until I discover his identity. I believe many of these stolen sisters are alive, and many more are dead and buried."

"Are we talking about Darcy's killer?" Treehorn asked.

"You're investigating two MMIW women, Darcy Clearwater and Sandy Begay. One murdered, one missing. Aren't we on the same team?"

"Of course."

"Darcy's murder differed from the others. Her body was left for you to find. The other victims are forever buried in unmarked graves."

"Do you think we have more than one killer?"

"The m.o. differs. I wonder why he dumped her body at that location."

Treehorn had made a note to himself about the body dump location, "How can we identify them?"

"Track Lakken's locations and the Missing and Murdered Indigenous Women."

"Do you think one of their employees is the killer and he's targeting women from violent homes to throw us off his trail?"

"Yes. I believe that. We don't have their bodies, but you have Darcy's. Your forensic coroner is extremely competent. She may find the one clue that will help you identify the killer."

"If you'll provide a list of the men who threatened Darcy and the MMIW, we can start there."

"I'll have Roni send it over."

Roni approached with a manila envelope. "I'm one step ahead of you, Jasper. You forget, I'm married to a State Trooper." The woman handed the packet to Agent Treehorn. "Here's the list of those who made threats and the specific threats themselves; and, I copied all the images from the awards dinner to a file for you."

"Thank you."

"You should give my husband a call. He keeps meticulous records for his job and he may be of help."

"Do either of you know if Darcy was dating anyone?"

Roni answered, "She wasn't dating anyone, to my knowledge."

Jasper hesitated, "I don't recall her mentioning anyone."

Treehorn sensed there was more to the retired agent's answer, "One last question, Mr. Redmond, why is your FBI record sealed?"

"That, Agent Treehorn, is none of your damn business." Jasper turned and walked away.

Roni waited until she heard Jasper's office door slam shut before she provided the answer to the men. "He put his time in, Agent Treehorn, and he retired from the FBI. I want to show you someone." Roni walked to the wall of *Stolen Sisters* and pointed to a beautiful red-headed teenager,

"This is Hanna Redmond, Jasper's only child. This image was taken when she was seventeen. She dated a Lakken Energy employee without her father's permission. She disappeared from here two years ago, along with the man. He took his pension, moved here, searched for her, and he swore he would never leave here until he found her, dead or alive."

"I apologize. I didn't know."

"Now, you do."

"One last thing, Darcy's cell phone is missing. Did anyone turn one in?"

"I thought you Feds were sharp. My husband already asked. I checked the premises and our lost and found. No luck. I recall Darcy was examining her phone right before she left. I thought it was odd, since we have limited service. She may have taken pictures with it."

"Do you have any questions for us?"

Roni examined the board. "See this woman?"

Treehorn and Raven examined the image of an Indian in her late forties.

"This is Nichelle Walters. She was found on the side of the road in Fort Peck, west of here. The Montana Highway Patrol found her alone in her car. Coroner ruled the death accidental, the cause alcohol poisoning."

Treehorn's criminal intuition asked, "You suspect otherwise?"

"Yes. Mrs. Walters was the Indian who killed Robert Beltram's wife, Brenda, while driving under the influence."

"What was the conclusion?" Raven wanted the details.

"Her family asked Jasper for help, but he had no legal standing. He made a few calls, but everyone was too busy with other Lakken crimes. Nichelle was sober after the fatality and until the day she died. I don't believe in coincidence, Agent Treehorn, and neither does my husband. Her body was found in the exact location of Brenda's fatal car accident."

"Why do you believe it was foul play instead of alcoholism?" Treehorn asked.

Roni shook her head, "It was too strange a coincidence that the now-sober Indian responsible for Brenda's death should die from an alcohol-related death on Brenda Beltram's birthday."

The agent handed Roni his business card. "Thank you for your time and all of the documents. We'll examine her file too."

Treehorn examined the *Stolen Sisters* one last time and observed that Darcy Clearwater's and Sandy Begay's photos were pinned next to red-haired Hanna Redmond's picture, whose sea-green eyes danced with merriment as she smiled for the photographer. He hoped someone would see those eyes again.

He and Raven retrieved their coats and continued their discussion of the investigation as they drove away from the community center. Treehorn ordered Raven to focus on detailed crimes affecting Lakken employees and the women. "Contact Bobby Beltram for the employees who had a problem with Darcy, cross reference them with the MMIW list, and see if there are any matches."

"I'll run all of them through the database for bad people doing bad things."

Treehorn frowned.

Raven saw his friend focus, "Is something else going on here?"

"I think we've determined the crimes that occurred here against women haven't been properly investigated."

"They lack the manpower and resources. The LEOs prioritized the serious crimes first," Raven stated in observation.

"Check for criminal history and crimes across state lines. Then, check with the Royal Canadian Mounted Police for their criminal printouts."

"You think they work for Lakken Energy and are involved in more widespread crime?" Raven's investigative mind didn't process information as fast as Treehorn's. He was better at research. Treehorn examined the criminal's behaviors and their causations. His instincts were telling him something larger and eviler was being perpetrated here.

Raven continued with his notes, "I'll pull Lakken telephone records and reconfirm the emergency call-out and records from the community center landlines. I'll see if we get lucky with any of the calls."

"Get a warrant for all of Lakken Energy's cell tower record transmissions and internet providers for them. Concentrate from 5 pm until 6 am on the day of Darcy's death. See who telephoned the community center. Let me know if you need help and I'll pull an agent for you."

"I'll ask if I need help," Raven continued to write notes.

"Process the photographs from the MMIW banquet. See if anything stands out of the ordinary. Enlarge Darcy's, Sandy's, and Hanna's images."

"What are you going to do?"

"I want a copy of Darcy's prescriptions from the pharmacy. I'll think about the investigation as I walk back to the office," Treehorn stated as he parked the vehicle at the pharmacy. He removed Bobby Beltram's business card and handed it to Raven, who copied the three numbers from the back.

"I'll pull them, too," Raven returned the card to Treehorn. He knew why his fellow agent requested their numbers. Everyone was a suspect.

"I want you to pull Brenda Beltram's and Nichelle Walter's investigations and have Dr. Reynolds pull their autopsies."

"You want to re-examine them?"

"It won't do any harm to take a look," Treehorn suggested.

Raven figured this was a good time to broach another subject, "John."

Treehorn stilled and cut the engine. His friend never used his first name and he refused to look at Raven, "What?"

Raven hesitated. "Dr. Reynolds."

Treehorn's left hand gripped the steering wheel as he stared at his wedding ring, "What about her?" He braced his bones for the reply.

"Skyler would be happy for you."

Treehorn thought of his dead wife as he sat with his friend in silence. The pain wasn't as sharp as in the past

107

when he heard her name and knew his friend's words came from the heart.

"Thank you."

Raven moved on, "So, where do we find Sandy Begay?"

"We find the connection between Darcy Clearwater and Sandy Begay. Someone has Sandy and we have her dress."

Chapter Seven

The crack of the whip. The smell of her blood. No red dress could conceal the bleeding welts that covered Sandy Begay's body from head to toe. The more she screamed and begged, the more he beat her with the whip, with his fists. His mother's voice echoed in his head. It told him how worthless he was. Well, he'd show her. His fists pounded the voices back until they retreated, until the ribs broke beneath his fists, until he silenced them, *for now.*

Williston Drugstore

Treehorn found the Williston Drugstore pharmacist during his lunch hour and presented the legal document with his badge and credentials to obtain Darcy's pharmacy records.

"FBI Special Agent John Treehorn. I'm investigating the death of Darcy Clearwater. I have a subpoena for her medication list." He handed the document to Mr. I. B. Taylor who read the official document.

"Just give me a minute to clear this with our legal department."

"On a separate matter, do you have a drug abuse problem with opiates in this area?"

"We dispense higher amounts, per capita, due to the oil energy industry and the physical labor required for the jobs. We take part in an opiate monitoring system, but we find that the majority of people who abuse opiates here have a physical injury that's been left untreated. It's usually due to the lack of health insurance or problems with workers compensation. Address that, Agent Treehorn, and you'll decrease opiate usage a good percent. If there's nothing else, I'll give the lawyer a call and page you when I have this information ready for you."

"Thanks."

Treehorn browsed the pharmacy while he waited. Large bandages, first aid supplies, and over-the-counter pain relievers lined a couple of aisles to address the needs of the energy workers. Another aisle was dedicated to birth control and sexual wellness items.

Just My Number surprised Treehorn as he examined the condom display. "You don't get out much, do you, Agent Treehorn?" She pointed to a popular brand, "That's a good make and model for your test drive."

Treehorn took a hard look at the young woman dressed in jeans, sweater, and minimal makeup. Her body language presented a youthful vitality, but her eyes showed a sad wariness.

She sensed Treehorn understood her. "I'm sure they have your size, they're labeled PRICK."

Treehorn lips lifted, "Do you still have my card?"

She ignored his question. "Do you want to bring your purchase over to my place and check their quality?"

"No. Do you have my card?" Treehorn asked again.

"Yes-I-do, Mr. Special Agent."

"This town is bad news for a hard-working girl like you. I'll help you get out of here, right now, if you want."

"I've made my plans. I'll leave when I'm good and ready."

"Sometimes bad things happen to women when they least expect it. Let me help you."

"The only offer on the table today, *John*, is my back pressed on one and you standing between my legs."

The loudspeaker activated with a man's voice, "Mr. Treehorn, please report to the pharmacy."

The agent's lips pursed in displeasure. "Call me, and I'll help you leave," he offered again.

Just My Number glanced at the condoms held in Treehorn's hand, smirked, and leaned into his space, "Call me, and I'll help you."

Treehorn heard her laughter as he walked to the pharmacist counter to pay for his supplies.

An attractive cashier examined his purchase, and then, him.

He paid with no comment.

The pharmacist approached the agent with the required paperwork, "Please fill in your name, badge number, and contact information."

Treehorn completed the form as requested and returned it to Mr. Taylor, who examined it for completeness, appeared satisfied, and handed the agent a single printout, "Do you have any questions?"

Treehorn read the sheet of paper; it listed the victim's diagnosis and corresponding medication. He had no questions; the facts were evident. "Thank you." Treehorn departed the drug store with another question and his purchase.

The two-mile walk to the FBI field office gave Treehorn the opportunity to speculate on the investigation. Dressed in his black woolen dress coat over his suit and tie made him stand out like the FBI agent he was. Several Lakken Energy wildcatters crowded him on the sidewalk and eyeballed him. Treehorn stared right back at the men. He knew someone from the company had an ax to grind with him. The question was, who?

Upon arriving at the office, Raven was busy with what he did best. Crime scenes photos now covered the bulletin board and he was on the phone, accessing Darcy's telephone records. He pointed to the counter where a lunch delivery sat for Treehorn.

The agent re-examined Darcy's apartment photos as he ate, focusing on the corner of her desk and the Trident award from the MMIW. Pinned to the upper corner was the folded copy of the *Indian Times* newspaper that pictured Treehorn, Raven, and Samuel Bear. Why had Darcy pinned that photo to her own bulletin board?

Raven had added a second bulletin board with maps of the Lakken Energy locations and the local area map, including the Fort Berthold and Fort Peck Indian Reservations, and neighboring lands where energy companies weren't allowed to drill. The agent had also attached Hanna Redmond's photo next to the maps.

When Raven finished his call Treehorn asked, "Did you pull Hanna Redmond's file?"

"Already done. I'm downloading Lakken Energy's history and files, and their history with the Feds, including the MMIW. The map will have pins where women were reported missing and the distance to their locations. I'll cross reference it with their employees."

"Good job, Raven."

"I'm also pulling the Lakken Energy contracts with the government to see if everything is up to date on their reports and financials."

"Buckman's been here long enough to know the dynamics of this town, including the money and its abuse. Check with the all of the police agencies for their records that cover these locations," Treehorn added.

Raven asked, "Is there something specific I should examine?"

"We know the major crime priorities assigned to LEOs. Let's look past that at some of the ones that haven't been thoroughly investigated."

"I'll get right on that," the agent added.

"I need to speak to Trooper Allen on a different matter," Treehorn added as he examined the crime scene photos of Darcy's apartment.

Raven saw Dr. Samantha Reynolds arrive at the office reception area. He watched his friend and fellow agent as he concentrated on his work. His co-worker had been blessed with exceptional investigative skills. The same skill witnessed time after time and admired on their joint cases.

Raven watched Samantha as she arrived at their door, and he turned to observe Treehorn's unguarded response.

"Hello," Samantha said.

Raven watched Treehorn's face redden. The man, who showed no emotion, was blindsided by a woman's voice.

Treehorn cleared his throat, "Hello. Come in." He felt Raven's stare and didn't look his way for confirmation.

"Good afternoon, Doc." Raven stood up and grabbed his empty coffee cup. "How are you today?"

"A little tired, but it's the nature of our profession."

"Would you like some coffee? I'm going for a refill."

"No thanks, Agent Shelly. I think I've had too much."

Raven walked out with his coffee mug as he whistled Ennio Morricone's, *The Good, The Bad, and The Ugly*'.

"He's a talented whistler," Samantha commented.

Treehorn chuckled. "Yes, and he increases his repertoire every time we work together. Would you like some water?" Treehorn offered.

115

Samantha nodded and Treehorn handed her a cold bottle from their tiny refrigerator. A fresh pot of coffee sat on the counter.

"Is the coffee better at a different pot?"

Treehorn smiled. "He's considerate of our privacy."

Samantha smiled as she checked out their office set up including the victim's bulletin boards. "Nice visuals. I've set up files on my computer on cases that have intrigued me."

"It's my methodology. I do the visuals, Raven excels at the research."

Samantha's nostrils flared when she neared Treehorn. His unique and subtle musky scent touched her senses. She smiled.

"What's funny?"

"Your musky, woodsy scent. It's unique."

Treehorn smelled his armpit.

She laughed, "I did a paper at Quantico on body scents."

"Did it stink?" Treehorn replied with his rapier wit.

She laughed again, "A-minus. I'll let you read it one day."

"I'd like that."

Samantha examined his office and his work board. "Do you set up a bulletin board for every investigation?" Samantha examined the victims and details.

"Yes. Facts."

Samantha handed him a document. "Here's a copy of Sandy Begay's DNA found on the dress Darcy was wearing. I've never had a homicide victim come in wearing a missing person's dress."

"I don't want to theorize. There's a pattern to the Missing and Murdered Indigenous Women. Their bodies don't turn up whereas Darcy's appeared to be intentionally placed to be found. I sense there's more to this dress than we know. I'm hoping it'll identify the killer."

Samantha handed Treehorn the second document "The second result—"

"—Darcy was pregnant," Treehorn completed her sentence.

"How'd you know before the lab results?"

"I visited the pharmacy. She had a prescription for prenatal vitamins."

"The semen samples were from two different men. The DNA from the vaginal sample was the father of the fetus. I used the University of Arizona DNA lab analysis for a quick turnaround."

"What about the second sample?"

"The lab is reprocessing it. They found a contamination discrepancy in the first sample, so they're retesting a second sample. I'm hoping those results will be available tomorrow. I'll run it through the Combined DNA Index System when it's returned."

"She may have had consensual sex with two partners. Was the second man her killer or another lover?"

Samantha blushed. The word sex caused both of them to focus on their awareness of each other.

"Why did you come here instead of calling?"

She whispered, "I wanted to see you."

He stepped forward and gently pushed Samantha back away from the office viewing and placed his hands gently on her face.

"May I?"

Her dilated pupils went from Treehorn's brown-blue eyes to his kissable lips. She gave the smallest nod and her eyes begged for it, for the normalcy of it.

The first soft joining of their lips tasted like bliss.

Her sigh added fire to Treehorn's desire.

He deepened the kiss, his tongue searching for hers, and that's when Treehorn felt her body stiffen in rejection, panic dilating her eyes.

"Excuse me," Raven interrupted.

The two jumped apart like guilty teenagers.

Samantha stuttered, "I have to get back to work. I'll keep you posted on any results."

Treehorn watched as she walked away. His angry eyes turned on Raven.

"Women!" Raven stated as he took a sip of his coffee.

"Shut up, Raven."

"I have to say, it's nice, my friend, that you've taken an interest in a woman."

"Shut up, Raven."

"She has a nice ass."

Treehorn placed his hand on his friend's shoulder and squeezed hard. "If you say another word, I'll give you a fat lip."

Raven was on thin ice, so he resisted, because Treehorn never stopped at a threat. He bit his tongue, stayed quiet, and rubbed his bruised shoulder.

"Darcy was pregnant, and we have the DNA results from the dress."

"The lab's results connect the two cases."

"We find Darcy's killer and we may find Sandy's kidnapper."

"Man, I hope she's still alive."

Treehorn texted Samantha, *"Dinner?"*

Samantha replied, *"No."*

"I'm sorry."

"Me too. Who's the father of Darcy's baby?"

Treehorn answered, but it wasn't what Samantha expected: *"Her husband."*

Treehorn telephoned Trooper Allen, "I need a favor."

Darcy Clearwater's Apartment

Trooper Allen's cruiser swung by Darcy's apartment at the agreed upon time between himself, his deputy watchman, and the agent.

Treehorn entered the darkened apartment from the unlocked rear door. He watched as the guard examined his timepiece, gathered his belongings, and departed for home. The agent sat in the comfortable chair next to the window. He watched the lightning illuminate the distant sky as the phenomenon known as thundersnow occurred out on the prairie. The wind-driven snow arrived with a white, unspoiled dusting from the spirits in an attempt to cover the dirt of the town. He sat and waited. It provided some comfort to him. He knew Darcy's husband would arrive tonight to take the one item in the apartment that would identify him.

As he sat and watched the snow fall, he thought of Samantha. It had been a long time since Treehorn had felt a taste of a woman's lips against his.

His eyes adjusted to the darkened apartment. The street light provided just enough illumination so he could identify the individual. He knew someone would come. The husband hadn't been able to collect it because the state troopers had assigned a deputy to watch the apartment. The Crime Scene Unit had descended on the apartment which prevented the inhabitant from scrubbing the apartment. He knew CSU had gathered his DNA from his scattered personal items. Treehorn knew he would come and collect the one item that only a Native American noticed and this would be the first opportunity for Darcy's husband to appear. It may be the only time Treehorn could identify and interrogate the man.

Treehorn sat for almost two hours and, then, he heard it, the arrival of a vehicle.

The headlights shut off, but no one stepped out from the vehicle. The windshield wipers cleaned the glass of snow and gave the agent a view of the occupant. Treehorn watched as the man inside the SUV took a long drink from a liquor bottle. His shoulders shook. It appeared that the grown man cried as he slumped over the steering wheel. He emptied the liquor bottle and grabbed a paper bag from the vehicle's front seat. Treehorn watched as he staggered out of the vehicle and approached the rear door, unlocked it after a couple attempts, stumbled into the room, and banged the door shut. Treehorn held his service weapon until he confirmed the identity of the man. He watched as the man staggered around the apartment without turning on the lights. As the man aimed for the bed, Treehorn broke the silence with a simple question, "Why did you lie to me when I asked if you were dating?"

The man stopped in his tracks. "I didn't lie to you, Agent Treehorn. Darcy and I weren't dating."

Treehorn turned on the lamp and holstered his weapon.

Bobby Beltram stood in front of him in his disheveled suit and alcohol breath. "We were married." He collapsed on the bed and bawled like a broken man who had lost his world. Treehorn knew the feeling; it had been the same for him when his wife was murdered.

Bobby pulled a fifth of whisky from his pocket and drank a large quantity. He tossed it aside and pulled another from his jacket. "I was with her at the awards ceremony. I was so proud of her. She's helped so many women." Bobby pulled a chain out from beneath his shirt. It held an intricate wedding band. "We were married six weeks ago. She made my ring. I gave her my mother's." He took a swig from the liquor bottle.

"Who would want her dead?" Treehorn asked.

"I don't know. My employees harassed her all the time. I felt like a referee most of the time. She wouldn't stop helping the abused women. I asked her once to stop, and do you know what she said? That, by not helping the victims, I was part of the problem. She was right." The liquor bottle was emptying fast. "She would still be alive if I hadn't gone to fight the well fire that night. When the police told me that she'd been murdered I felt like I had died, too. I went to the morgue to identify her and I hoped that someone had the wrong body."

"I'm sorry."

"She was my forever…." Bobby cried.

Treehorn needed answers. "Have you located her computer or phone?"

"No, she had her phone at the ceremony. She was taking my picture. Her computer had just work reports, nothing top secret, and"—Bobby cried— "our wedding video." The man turned green, "I'm going to be sick." He rushed to the toilet where the expensive Scotch ended its journey.

Treehorn waited.

Bobby washed and returned to the bed, worse for wear. His voice slurred, "Can you find who killed her, so I can kill them?"

Treehorn vowed, "I'll find her killer and we'll let the justice system work."

"Can you find her wedding ring?" Bobby asked as he slowly passed out on the bed clutching his own wedding ring to his chest. "My father didn't know we were married."

The agent watched as Bobby passed out. He didn't want to be the one to inform the widower that Darcy had been pregnant at the time of her death. He knew it wouldn't help the investigation, and once Bobby knew his wife was with child, he would carry the sadness with him every day of his life until the Great Spirit claimed him.

Treehorn knew this because his wife had been pregnant when she died.

He needed a drink.

Chapter Eight

Treehorn walked into the bar, using his ingrained law enforcement observation skills to scope out the interior. Locals sat on the left and the oil field workers sat on the right. He felt the atmosphere shift when he entered. He received a few nods from the patrons. Word gets around real quick in a town when a long-time, local resident is murdered. The room's occupants knew he was a federal agent. Conversations resumed by the time Treehorn reached the bar and ordered his drink. He took his beer and found a seat at an empty table that sat dead-center in the room. The beer went down fast and smooth. By the time he lowered the bottle to the wooden surface, a waitress had materialized.

"Would you like another?"

"Bring a couple but leave the bottles, please." A man knew how to count his limitations.

A sudden drift of her perfume identified the arrival of Just My Number.

"Hello, Agent Prick." She didn't bother asking if Treehorn wanted her company as she took a seat next to him, too close in fact.

"Quiet night?"

"I'm hoping to get lucky with a *john*."

The bar patrons took notice of the FBI agent and hooker, and so did Agent Donovan who hid in the darkened corner of the room while he readied his smart phone.

"Did you open your purchase yet?"

"Not your business."

"When was the last time you had company?" Just My Number rubbed his thigh with her manicured nails.

Treehorn grabbed her hand and placed it on the table.

Donovan snapped a picture of the interaction of the two at the table.

"What's your name, Just My Number?"

"That'll cost you."

The arrival of the waitress prevented a reply. Treehorn paid and tipped her. The bar staff assumed they were together and placed Treehorn's second beer in front of his unwelcome guest.

"Have a beer, Just My Number." Treehorn chugged his drink.

"It's Janie Marie Nettles."

Treehorn acknowledged with a nod.

"Are you gay? Bi? Kinky? I can play good cop, bad cop." She teased.

"No. I'm an FBI agent who's always on duty."

"Wow, the job over the wife."

The hooker felt the chill and knew that subject wouldn't be repeated.

Agent Donovan watched the pair interact.

"Tell me about this town."

"That'll cost you, and I don't take credit."

He ignored her negotiation, "Tell me about Lakken, the girls, and the abuse."

"How much time do we have? The Greyhound bus arrives every day. Girls come hoping for a better life. We never think too long about anything bad happening to us. Then we hear another girl has disappeared and we hoped she hopped back on the bus and got the hell out of here."

"Do you have any family?"

"I have a sister in Fargo."

"Do you want me to put your ass on the bus?"

"No. I'm doing okay here. I have a roof over my head and a job on my back, and I paid my water bill today, Agent Treehorn. I'm living the American Dream."

Treehorn removed a hundred-dollar bill from his wallet and stuffed it into Janie's bag.

"No back work tonight."

Agent Donovan recorded the cash transaction, almost as if it was planned.

"I'll put it in my travel fund."

"It's good that you have one."

Just My Number watched Treehorn drink his beer and wished she'd met this man in a previous lifetime.

"Did you know Darcy Clearwater, the engineer who was murdered?"

Janie nodded, "Yeah, I knew her. She helped girls escape from here."

"Who didn't take kindly to her activities?"

"Lakken Energy."

"Can you be more specific?"

"Brody Hauler. Crew leader for the company. Mean son of a bitch. Most of the girls avoided him." Janie searched among the wildcatters. Brody Hauler wasn't hard to locate. He was a tall, black-haired, scarred man holding court in a corner. A hooker sat on his lap while his hand was busy beneath her dress.

"He's the guy in the corner holding the girl in the red sequined dress."

Treehorn glanced toward the corner. "And, when they can't avoid him?"

"They do what he asks because, if they don't, they may turn up dead."

"Why do you say that?"

"He's here to crew his men. The harder his men work, the more money they bring in for Lakken. When his men aren't working, they're drinking and whoring."

Treehorn watched the man dump the girl into a chair and walk toward the restroom. The worker felt Treehorn's eyes and turned a dead stare toward him. Both men sized each other up. Brody was the first to break his stink-eye contact when he disappeared behind a dividing wall.

The agent wasn't privy to Brody's short discussion with Agent Donovan, who remained hidden in the shadows.

Janie brought Treehorn's attention back to her. "Agent Treehorn, the bottom line is you adapt here, or you die here. It's the town. I need to go to the ladies' room. I'll tell you more when I return."

The waitress approached and delivered two more beers. He paid and tipped the hard-working girl. Treehorn sipped this beer as he examined the crowd and noticed on the noisier side of the joint, the oil wildcatters enjoyed harassing the waitresses. The locals, on the other side of the beer joint, were quieter. It was as if an invisible line separated the two and Treehorn's table was that dividing marker. He looked more closely at the patrons and identified several LEOs drinking with their partners.

Treehorn watched as Brody Hauler spoke with a Lakken man near the restroom. That man approached three other workers, who all stared at Treehorn. Then, all four men approached Treehorn's table in an attempt at group intimidation.

The crowd quieted as if the men had violated bar room etiquette.

"It's time for you to leave."

Treehorn eyed the four men. "I'm not done with my drink."

The man who had spoken first grabbed the agent's beer and emptied the remaining contents onto Treehorn's lap.

"You're done now."

Treehorn stood. He had six inches on all the men, but four against one wasn't good odds when the others were mean and muscular.

"What's your name?"

"Why, are you going to arrest me for spilling your drink?" The men laughed.

"No, I want to know what name to put on the ambulance report." Treehorn punched the man in his jaw and he went down for the count.

The remaining three surprised men, without a plan, rushed Treehorn.

One man bloodied the agent's lip, and he responded with a drop-kick to the man's groin, rendering him useless. The other two men went for Treehorn, but each received blackened eyes with possible broken noses in their feeble attempts.

"Enough." The three conscious men froze on Brody Hauler's order. They watched as the crew leader poured his own drink on the unconscious fourth, who sputtered awake. "Get out." They would be paid for their loyalty, but not in front of the Fed.

The two men assisted their injured friends in their hasty retreat.

Three fresh wildcatters lined up behind Brody Hauler. "What's it going to take for you to understand that you're not welcome here?" Arrogance laced the sarcasm.

Treehorn watched as three LEOs formed a protective detail behind him.

Brody didn't expect an answer from the Fed, so he turned to walk away.

"Pussy." Everyone heard Treehorn's cat call.

Brody stopped in his tracks, his back rigid.

The agent watched as the crew leaders' hands clenched into fists.

"You and your boys want a fight?" Brody asked without any worry of being defeated.

Treehorn looked at the three men behind him for a consensus. He recognized two FBI agents and a state trooper. The men nodded.

"If it's fair."

The bar patrons waited for his response.

"Yes." Brody beckoned the waitress to bring the boxes.

"The waitress will explain the rules."

She arrived carrying two lock boxes.

Treehorn was quick on the uptake; this was normal fight night.

The Lakken Energy men emptied the contents of their pockets into one of the boxes.

"Rule number one, one hundred dollars per man, to cover any damages."

Wallets, jackknives, keys, and cash landed inside the Lakken box.

Brody placed four hundred dollars on top of their belongings and the waitress locked it.

She turned to Treehorn and his men.

He opened his wallet and looked at his backup team, "I've got this."

An FBI agent stepped forward, "No, we've got this. It's long overdue," as he placed four hundred dollars in the officer's box.

The LEOs then added service weapons, badges, wallets, and keys.

The waitress locked the boxes and handed both of them to a muscular man who took them and guarded them on a table in plain sight.

"Rule number two, the bell starts it. Rule number three, the bell stops it."

Eight men waited for the bell to start their free-for-all brawl.

As the bell rang, Agent Donovan grabbed Janie Marie Nettles and hauled out the rear door. He gave her a hard shove toward his parked sedan.

"You did well. Now, I want your company."

"I don't want yours."

Agent Donovan grabbed her upper arm in a bruising grip through her wool jacket.

"You're hurting me."

"I'll hurt you more if you don't get in the car."

He opened the rear door of his cruiser and forced her inside. As he walked around the sedan, Janie activated a device in her purse.

"I was with him like you wanted, Agent Asshole."

Agent Donovan opened the rear door and backhanded Janie hard across the face.

"Did he pay to screw you?"

Janie rubbed her swollen cheek. "No, he didn't pay me for sex."

"Were you giving him a freebie?"

"No. He didn't want my services."

"Well, then, what did he want?"

"Information."

Agent Donovan squeezed her arm.

"You're hurting me."

"Be more specific."

"Why do you care?"

Agent Donovan raised his other hand to strike her.

Janie answered, "He asked about Darcy Clearwater."

"What did he want to know?"

"Like, if I knew her." Janie didn't elaborate further on their conversation.

"The next time you see him you will set him up as a paid john, do you understand?"

"I won't set up an innocent man."

Donovan slapped her again. "Yes, you will." He grabbed his handcuffs and secured her wrists to the security bar inside his cruiser.

"I want out right now."

"You'll get out when I tell you. I'm arresting your ass."

"For what?"

"I'll figure that out when I'm done with you."

When they arrived at her lodging, Agent Donovan released her from the handcuffs. While she searched for her house key inside her bag, she checked to see if her device was blinking red, unbeknownst to the dirty agent. Janie vowed this was the last night she would spend time with this asshole. She couldn't have foreseen how true her promise would become.

The agent dragged her inside. Darcy Clearwater had helped Janie prepare for tonight. It was a night to celebrate.

Janie offered Agent Donovan a beer before he started his sexual assault on her for the last time.

The table was full of empty beer bottles that sat on top of the weapons box. Treehorn and the three LEOs were exchanging crime stories while they drank their beers to dull their injuries. Their bruised and swollen faces appeared more like the criminals they arrested than the epitome of law enforcement. FBI Agents Garrand and Wilson were holding cold beers to their eyes to prevent them from swelling shut, without much success. The trooper held an ice pack to his jaw. Treehorn held his cold beer to his right rib.

The waitress approached the table with a plastic recycling container to gather the empty beer bottles that covered the top of the table.

State Trooper Owens appeared to have fared better than the other LEOs.

The Fed asked him his secret.

"USMC Boxing Class of '93."

They all laughed, then their injuries made them regret that.

Treehorn handed the waitress a $100 tip. "Thanks for ringing the bell."

She smiled, "I rang it to save your asses."

Moans and groans echoed around the table.

"Did you see Janie tonight?" Treehorn wanted to make sure she was safe.

The waitress answered, "She left with one of her regulars."

Treehorn touched his jaw with his cold beer.

"Can I get you some ice?" The waitress took sympathy on him.

"I'd appreciate that."

"I called a taxi to transport you three back to your lodging." She looked at the trooper, "Your wife is waiting outside with her friends to drive your sorry ass home, and just to warn you, she's not happy."

The men stood and drained the last of the beers they held, gathered their weapons and possessions and staggered outdoors.

The waitress handed the agent a small bag of ice.

"Thanks."

Treehorn, along with Garrand and Wilson piled into the taxi.

"We may have won that round Agent Treehorn, but the men around here avoid Brody Hauler; and, I recommend that you do the same," Agent Garrand offered his recommendation.

"Why's that?" Treehorn questioned.

"He's a psychopath," Agent Wilson stated, matter-of-fact.

Agent Garrand provided the history, "A couple years ago there was a story that circulated of a local resident who was out hunting prairie dogs and trespassed on Lakken Energy land. Supposedly, the hunter watched through his binoculars and witnessed Brody as he raped a red-headed woman on the tailgate of his truck, then he shot her boyfriend. The man told no one what he had seen. He mailed a letter to the state police with the details but not a specific location, and they forwarded a copy to us."

"Was the hunter, boyfriend, or woman identified?" Treehorn asked.

Agent Garrand continued, "No, the hunter sent the letter anonymously and the troopers had no way to identify or follow up on the information. The man wrote in his letter he would not identify himself and become a target for a cold, hard killer."

Agent Wilson added, "Rumors spread. Brody stated if he ever heard any man repeating the lies that he'd throw them into a hole, put a bullet in their head, and cover them with stones so they would never be found, even by the hungriest wolf. The gossip stopped. No woman reported any rape with a shooting death."

"Case went cold," Agent Garrand summarized. "The workers believed if they spread gossip, they would end up dead. Fear and money keep them quiet. The company pays plenty for its loyalty."

"Men like that come from bad seeds. The apple never falls far from the tree," Agent Wilson concluded.

The taxi arrived at the FBI housing and the agents observed Samantha sitting outside with a heavy coat against the freezing temperatures.

"She's a cold one," Agent Garrand commented.

"She doesn't put out for any man," Agent Wilson stated.

"She's probably into pussy." Agent Garrand realized he crossed a line when he felt Treehorn's fist grab his collar.

"If you misogynist assholes ever disrespect a woman in front of me again, I'll have you reassigned to the worst shithole posting in the history of the FBI. Do you understand?" He whispered it, but they felt its impact like a hammer.

Agent Wilson dared to ask, "You….?" He choked when he saw the anger reflected in Treehorn's eyes as they bored into him.

The two agents didn't wait for a reply. They threw some money to the driver and stumbled out of the taxi in their rush to get away from their fellow agent.

Samantha watched the drunken men.

Agent Wilson avoided eye contact with Samantha, while Agent Garrand greeted her, "Hi, Doc."

"Gentleman, you're looking a little worse for wear."

"You should see the other guys!" The two agents laughed and stumbled to their rooms.

Treehorn waited for their doors to close. "What are you doing out here?"

Samantha moved the blanket from the bench and Treehorn took that as a silent offer to sit. She covered him with the blanket and moved her service revolver. Treehorn didn't comment on her security precautions.

"It's a good night to see the stars. I'm usually assigned to cities and never see the beauty of the night skies."

"Have either of them harassed you?"

"No, both of them asked me out, and I declined."

"Why did you say no?" The alcohol loosened Treehorn's tongue.

"They weren't you." Samantha smiled at the stars. "Can I get you a drink?"

"No thanks."

"Who was Darcy Clearwater's husband?" Samantha's mantra was *focus on the case, not Treehorn.*

"Bobby Beltram."

"How'd you figure that?"

"She had a Navajo Indian wedding basket hung in her bedroom. They're given to the couple on their wedding day to celebrate their life's journey. Earlier this evening, I waited at the apartment for him and he arrived, highly intoxicated."

Samantha countered, "He didn't say anything at the morgue when he identified her body. How's he doing?"

"His wife was murdered. He'll feel worse when he finds out she was pregnant."

"I'm sorry. I didn't mean it the way it came out."

Treehorn said, "My wife Skyler was pregnant when she was murdered." The only person who knew was his mother.

"I'm sorry. Why do you still wear your wedding ring?"

"The memories bring me comfort."

"Didn't you want to try to meet someone and move on?"

"No."

"Why not?" Samantha asked as she laid a comforting hand on his arm.

He shrugged it off, "Leave it alone."

"I want to help." Samantha looked deep into his eyes.

"Help? You're afraid of your own shadow."

"I'm not afraid of you."

"You should be."

He stood and lifted Samantha up from the bench, then lowered his lips to hers. He kissed her for the pain of his dead wife, he kissed her for the love that he lost, for the child he would never see born, and he kissed her for the hope he still found in one little corner of his broken heart. Samantha embraced it. He was broken, and she was broken. Two kindred spirits who somehow found each other.

Samantha's hands moved beneath his jacket and shirt to caress his skin. Her hands encountered scar tissue.

He stiffened.

"What happened?" Samantha moved her hands over his back.

He shrugged her hands off him. "You're not the only victim walking this land, Samantha."

"I know that."

Treehorn didn't turn around but removed his jacket and lifted his shirt and showed Samantha his scar-covered back. He refused to turn around to see the horror on her face like he had experienced from so many others. "I was there the day my wife was murdered. A man killed her and almost killed me, too." Treehorn lowered his shirt.

Samantha wrapped her arms around him from behind.

"How did you live with it?"

"You know the routine. Quantico recognized a trauma victim, a therapists assigned, I dealt with the issues to their satisfaction, the staff signed off, and I became an FBI agent."

"Have you been alone since your wife's death?"

Treehorn removed her arms from him. "How do you define alone? The therapist signed off my case, so that she could engage in a sexual relationship with me and still keep her license."

"You dated your therapist?"

"No, Samantha, I screwed her. There's a difference."

Samantha rubbed her lips. "Why did you kiss me, if you're involved with someone?"

"The attraction isn't one-sided." Treehorn stepped away.

"Does it get any easier?" Samantha whispered.

"Has it for you?" Treehorn continued toward his lodging.

Samantha yelled at his back, "I was raped, Agent Treehorn. It's never gotten easier."

Treehorn stopped and looked over his shoulder, "I was assaulted too. I know what it's like to be a victim and a victim never forgets."

Samantha's eyes widened in horror and her face reddened in shame. "I'm sorry." Only she heard the whispered words.

Chapter Nine

Brody Hauler sat drinking a six-pack in his pickup truck. He strategically parked his red truck amongst the other vehicles in the parking lot across from the FBI lodging. Between beers he watched as Treehorn arrived with the two other FBI agents. Two agents staggered away. He observed Treehorn's interaction with the medical examiner. Then, he saw the Fed kiss her. He would make that prick pay for the beating he received, and now, he knew how. Brody dialed his cell phone, and it was hard to talk through his broken tooth and bruised jaw, "Tell me everything you know about FBI Agent Treehorn."

Brody Hauler drove home. The beer didn't soothe the ache. He knew the agent was trouble; he would have to plan something to keep him busy and out of his hair. The voices in his head whispered, *"He'll figure it out…he'll figure it out…he'll figure it out."* The mantra didn't stop.

When he arrived home, he opened the door to his windowless room, the little sixteen by eight-foot prison where he kept them, all of them, without anyone ever knowing. The women's voices begged, begged just like his pathetic whore of a mother. It became the same voice of the demon that had danced in his head since the day his mother assaulted him. *"He'll figure it out."*

He bent her over the table. "TELL-ME-YOU'RE-SORRY-MOTHER!" Brody screamed. She begged, she resisted, she fought, and then she whispered, "I'm sorry." He squeezed her neck until his body exploded and the voices stopped. He changed his clothes and celebrated with another cold beer.

Agent Donovan finished his beer and threw the bottle at Janie who crouched and whimpered in the corner. He showered and dressed so he didn't smell like a whore for his unsuspecting wife. He counted off five Ben Franklins from his money clip. It wasn't his cash; he'd removed it from a drug dealer's dead body. He unlocked his handcuffs from Janie's wrists, found his car keys, and left her sniveling and slightly banged-up body in the corner. Donovan whistled as he swung his handcuffs in rhythm to his song.

Janie vowed she would stick to the plan Darcy had arranged. A very meticulous plan because in less than eight hours the dirty agent would be wearing his handcuffs and Janie knew she had his number.

Brody unlocked the pair of handcuffs that had encased the pale wrists covered with blackened bruises, cuts, and dried blood, "Sorry, I was a little rough there." He gently caressed her face. The petechial hemorrhages of her lifeless eyes and the emerging finger imprints around her neck could be diagnosed by a first-day medical student. He grabbed her naked lifeless body around her ribs and carried her from his dark dungeon, across his kitchen floor, through his back door, and dumped her into the rear of his pickup truck. He returned inside and grabbed a red dress. Brody slammed down his truck cover, gunned the engine, and sped away.

He had a present for Agent Treehorn.

Janie watched as Agent Donovan drove away. She stood up, locked her apartment door, and knew she had survived. The hidden video camera recorded every bruise and bite mark on her body left by Agent Asshole as she slowly turned around for its documentation.

She pulled out a United States Postal Service box that was addressed to FBI Supervisor Louise Buckman and emptied its contents onto her table. She stripped the linen off her bed and inserted it into its specially-marked plastic bag. The used condoms were retrieved from the bathroom and placed in evidence bags. All the contents were then meticulously tagged, as if she had planned everything ahead of time, which she had with Darcy's help.

Janie proceeded with the collecting of samples for the prosecution that were on a list, and she followed it exactly. She took detailed photographs of her bruises with her digital camera and labeled the memory chip before inserting it into the mailer. Janie retrieved the audio recording from her purse taken at the bar when Agent Donovan forced her into his cruiser. She added the five hundred dollar bills he had paid her with into an additional evidence bag and labeled it, "Payment for Prostitution by FBI Agent Dennis Donovan." Finally, she opened the wall mirror that hid the secret video recording machine. She pushed the "Stop Recording" button, removed the video tape, placed it into its holder, and inserted it into the postage box. The video tape had activated its recording when she passed the sensor in her bedroom; what seemed like a lifetime ago. She would have loved to see the man in handcuffs but would have to be satisfied reading it in the *Indian Times* newspaper.

The last things she placed inside the postage box were two letters. One addressed to L. Buckman and the other to Special Agent John Treehorn. She couldn't thank him enough for helping her get out of the business. She hoped, one day, he would know. Sometimes all it takes is one person to believe in you to make a difference. She took a long hot shower, dressed, packed her suitcase, and grabbed her knapsack. She departed this life wearing her favorite piece of clothing, a long red satin dress under her short winter jacket.

Brody backed his truck across the culvert. There were no headlights coming from either direction. He opened the tailgate of his truck, pulled the body to the edge, and removed the red satin dress. He climbed the hill to the tree and tied the dress to its lower limb. Brody suspected that Jasper Redmond had visited the site for the Missing and Murdered Indigenous Women's movement and had hung a red dress labeled "MMIW." Brody hung his article of clothing next to it to make a point. He searched his pockets and found his working marker. He wrote a name on the MMIW dress. Brody returned to his truck and with no traffic on the horizon he pulled the body out, and dumped her face-down, naked, and positioned her inside Darcy Clearwater's yellow police crime scene ribbon. He removed his jackknife from his pocket and carved two words into Sandy's buttocks. He wiped the blade in the snow and pocketed it. Brody closed the truck's tailgate, gunned the

149

engine, and spun the tires as his V-8 roared down the road. A mile from the body dump, Brody passed a wolf sitting on the edge of the road. He would have sworn, on his mother's grave, the same wolf had spoken, *"He'll figure it out."* It was now a tune Brody couldn't get out of his head.

Janie walked to the post office and deposited her pre-stamped box into the chute. Agent Donovan's termination countdown as a federal agent had officially begun. Janie jumped up on their park bench and laughed out loud. It felt great to finally feel free. Thankfully, no one saw or heard her. She glanced at her watch and realized she had plenty of time to catch her shuttle bus to Fargo. She sat down and smiled. Her sister would see her tomorrow, but first she had to walk to the bus terminal. She grabbed her suitcase, smiled, and aimed for the street.

At the same time, a passing driver saw her red satin dress illuminated by the lights of the parking area.

Brody Hauler slammed on his brakes, reversed, and drove into the post office parking lot. He stopped next to Janie and her luggage. Brody rolled down his window. "Going someplace, Janie?"

"I'm visiting my sister in Fargo." She shifted from foot to foot in her leather shoes that had kept her feet dry in the snowy slush but which she now realized weren't made for walking.

"I don't think those shoes will make it!" Brody looked at the slim ankles encased in leather, his view traveled up her legs, and wondered what her breasts would feel like squeezed, "Hop in, I'll give you a ride to the bus station."

Janie's feet hurt and there were limited taxis at night. "Sure. I'd appreciate that." Brody got out of his truck and placed her suitcase and knapsack behind his seat and helped her into the passenger seat and fastened her seatbelt. He returned to the driver's seat and looked at Janie's beautiful eyes and said, "My mother always wore red dresses like yours. You look as beautiful as she did. Thanks for the memory."

"I'm sorry, is she dead?"

Brody thought of an answer; it wasn't as if she would repeat it, "Yes, she's dead. I dug a hole next to a tree, beat the crap out of her, and buried her alive when I was sixteen." He laughed. Janie's hand grabbed the door release handle at the same time his fist struck her jaw with a knockout blow.

151

When she regained consciousness, she knew how Brody felt when Treehorn had delivered a knockout blow to him earlier that evening during the bar fight.

His jaw hurt. A long hot shower washed away the sweat but did little to ease the tension in Treehorn. He tried focusing on Darcy's murder and Bobby Beltram's involvement. What was the motive for her death? He dressed in a clean T-shirt and boxers. His lip throbbed and his ribs hurt. His bruised knuckles provided proof they had found their mark on Brody Hauler's jaw and body. Was Brody capable of murder? The agent believed any man could commit murder if the circumstances were right. That was his last thought before sleep claimed him.

Samantha showered and dressed in her T-shirt and plaid pajamas. She rechecked the lock on her door for the second time and sat by the window, looking out at the darkness and thinking about Treehorn. What was it about him that made her want to come out of her shell and try to live again? She closed her eyes and touched her lips. She could still feel his taste on her. She felt her heart as it raced, not in a panic, but with excitement. Her therapist told her that life would be better one day; all it would take for her was time and the right person.

Samantha crawled into bed and hugged the extra pillows. Would she ever feel the comfort of a man's arms holding her without having a panic attack? She wrapped the blankets tight around her and pretended that it was Treehorn's arms that held her as she fell asleep.

Trooper Allen sat in his patrol car finishing the last of his cold coffee and Cookie Lighthouse's gingersnaps. His clock showed 7:45 am, one hour fifteen minutes remained of his shift. Sunrise, a welcome sight at this time. It provided him with the energy to finish his detail.

His police radio snapped him to attention, "Car 1311. Trooper Allen, come in."

"1311 here." The patrol adjusted the volume of his radio.

"Car 1311, what's your 20?"

"I'm near MM 222, issuing tickets to unsuspecting speeders."

"Car 1311, Trooper Maresca just reported the tanker with license L-A-K-N-H-2-0 just passed MM 220 and is heading in your direction."

"Copy that."

"He's en route to your location to assist."

"10-4."

Allen placed his coffee in its holder next to his cookies and waited patiently for the tanker; the one driver that all the North Dakota State Troopers had searched for, the prick who had splashed him when he found Darcy Clearwater's body. He spotted the truck and watched it as it approached his active radar. The radar beeped and recorded the truck speeding 20 mph over the posted speed limit.

"Gotcha." He turned on his lights and siren and drove onto the tarmac to chase down the offender. Maresca turned on his lights and sirens too to offer help to his fellow LEO. The truck pulled over at MM 223, one mile short of the Darcy Clearwater's body dump site. That was the trooper's thought as he stomped through the snow with his new ticket book and fresh pen.

Maresca watched as his peer issued ticket after ticket to the speeding truck driver, one Winston Brooks, originally from Billings, who now resided in Williston. The officer would have issued more tickets but that would have been petty and would have delayed the end of their shift. The cop had one last question for the obnoxious and agitated truck driver, "Why do you haul water here?"

"I deliver it to the men out at the oil wells, they need fresh water. It pays my bills, and it's not against the law."

Allen handed the truck driver back his license and registration. "Break another law and you won't have a license to drive."

"Think he'll learn?" Maresca asked as they walked toward their cruisers.

Allen shook his head. "Congratulations on the Marshal Service."

"Thanks. The wife is happy to have us move closer to her family in DC."

The tanker started its smoky diesel engine and its driver ground its gears in a failed attempt at a hasty departure.

The police looked at each other and shook their heads.

"Thirty minutes left. I think I'll stay out here where it's quiet."

The warmth in the patrol car removed the chill of the North Dakota wind as Toby watched his co-worker depart. He radioed dispatch, "Car 1311 back in service."

"Dispatch 10-4."

He sat and enjoyed a minute of quiet solitude as he finished his coffee. Something moved in the distance, but the snow that blanketed the landscape and whipped by its winds reduced the trooper's visibility to a hundred yards. The policeman grabbed for his binoculars in their protective case and checked the horizon for a better view.

The wolf stared back at him and caused the hairs to stand up on the back of his neck. He turned the car heater up to maximum to take away the twin chill.

The trooper looked at the mileage sign outside his passenger side window, then at the desolate stretch of highway in front of his car. He thought about Agent Treehorn and the wolf. *Were they guiding him?* He shook his head at his absurd thoughts. *I'll turn around at the woman's body dump location and prove them both wrong.*

Treehorn and Raven entered the FBI office at 8am. Agent Donovan was in Buckman's office engaged in a very serious conversation. The agent handed his supervisor what appeared to be photographs. She examined them and started searching the office for someone. When her eyes landed on Treehorn she motioned for him to come to her office.

Agent Donovan crowded Treehorn as they passed at the supervisor's doorway. Buckman shouted, "Agents Garrand and Wilson. Get in here now."

The supervisor focused on Treehorn as she waited for her agents to appear. The Indian's cut lip and bruised face drew her attention. She'd bet the cup of coffee that sat on her desk that the other man had fared worse. She examined the faces of the two agents as they arrived. Their black eyes told their story. Three FBI agents, the worse for wear, stood at attention in front of her desk.

"Acclimating with the locals?"

"It was a fair fight," Agent Garrand stated.

"We followed bar rules," Agent Wilson tag-teamed him.

"Did I ask?" Buckman asked.

Treehorn stood straight, tall, and silent.

Buckman asked, "Do you wish to comment?"

"It was a fair fight, and we followed bar rules."

Agent Wilson smiled carefully through his cracked lip. Treehorn had their backs. He lost the grin when he caught his supervisor's eye.

"Get out." Buckman pointed to her door.

The agents turned to leave.

"Not you, Treehorn."

As the agents walked away, Buckman got in the last word, "You two need to improve your hand-to-hand combat skills gentlemen." They left the door wide open as they hastily departed.

"What were you doing with a prostitute last night, Agent Treehorn?" Buckman showed the man a photograph of him and Janie together.

Treehorn searched the outer offices and spotted Agent Donovan, who watched the show with a smirk on his face. Dr. Reynolds stood next to him, and from the distressed look on her face it was clear she overheard Buckman's question.

The agent closed Buckman's door without permission.

"I thought you were different, but it seems you've adapted well to this environment."

"I paid a prostitute for her time and for information. We didn't have sex. We sat at a bar and I questioned her about Darcy Clearwater. I was told she left later with one of her regulars. Photographs can be made to imply something. Nothing happened."

"Why is Agent Donovan gunning for you?"

Treehorn zoomed in on Donovan, again. "Good question."

"What actually happened to your face and those of my agents?"

"Lakken Energy boys picked a fight."

"Was it fair?"

"Yes." Treehorn wondered why she would believe him and not her own staff.

Buckman held up her hand, "I don't want to know anymore," She underestimated this agent, "Don't make me look like a fool; it's a look I don't like."

"I understand."

"Agent Donovan has a real hard-on for you." She lowered her voice. "I'm going to stand here and chew your ass out."

Treehorn gave a slight nod.

Buckman shouted at Treehorn, "Do you understand?"

Treehorn gave a big nod.

Everyone in the office heard Buckman through her closed door and observed Treehorn's response.

Agent Donovan flirted with Samantha, "Do you want to have a drink with me later since Treehorn prefers hookers?"

"One day, Agent Donovan, you're going to reap what you sow!"

Treehorn watched as Samantha didn't stay for the conclusion of Buckman's diatribe and stormed out of the building.

Chapter Ten

Trooper Allen stopped his patrol car a hundred feet from the previous crime scene location and turned off his engine. He focused on the lone tree, standing tall and proud on the hillside. And that's when he saw the two red dresses swinging from its limb. He wondered if the MMIW organization hung the dresses as a sign of respect for homicide victims. He sure hoped so; he didn't want the wolf to be right and him to be wrong.

He contacted dispatch, "Dispatch, car 1311 here."

"Dispatch. Go ahead 1311."

"I'm out of my car north of mile marker two-two-four. Checking on a possible wild animal sighting."

"Be careful, Trooper Allen."

"Roger that!"

Trooper Allen saw Darcy Clearwater's broken crime scene tape blowing in the brisk prairie wind as if it was waving for his attention.

The wolf was forgotten when he spotted the naked woman's body lying in the exact position as Darcy

Clearwater's body. He approached her and saw the open, lifeless eyes. Trooper Allen didn't need to feel for a pulse. His flashlight illuminated the strangulation marks around her neck in the early dawn light and he guessed her cause of death by the petechial hemorrhaging in her eyes.

He called the local dispatcher with his handheld radio, "Dispatch, Trooper Allen here,"

"Dispatch, go ahead 1311."

"I have another dead body at mile marker two-two-four."

"Can you repeat?" asked the operator.

"I have a dead body at mile marker two-two-four," Trooper Allen repeated.

"Toby, are you serious?" The dispatcher misplaced her professionalism.

"Yes, I'm serious. Notify the coroner, and patch me through to Louise Buckman, FBI." Trooper Allen ordered.

"Will do," dispatch concluded.

Trooper Allen removed his phone from its holder and snapped a picture of the woman's face. He pressed his phone button and sent the image to the coroner, labeled "DOA - female - MM 224 - possibly MP - Sandy Begay." He declined to inform the dispatcher of the condition of the victim's body. Every Williston law enforcement agency would soon be informed of this homicide and what some sick bastard did to her. She was covered in bruises and lacerations; but it was the knife cuts that sliced her rear that held Trooper Allen's attention, *"John Treehorn"* was carved into her buttocks.

Buckman finished berating Treehorn as her desk phone beeped.

Denise, her personal assistant interrupted her only on urgent matters, "Trooper Allen on line one."

She welcomed the diversion as she pressed the phone button. "Louise Buckman."

Treehorn searched the outer offices for Agent Donovan, but he was nowhere in sight.

"Where was the body found?" She listened to his reply. "Repeat that location."

The agent focused on Buckman's one-sided conversation.

"We'll be right there." She slammed the handset into its cradle. "Trooper Allen believes Raven Shelly's missing person just turned up and it's not pretty; dead with your name carved on her ass."

FBI Supervisor Buckman, her face red from the cold wind, watched her staff as they worked the crime scene. Her phone rang, and she listened to the urgent message. "I'll be right there."

Treehorn and Raven watched as her face darkened in anger.

She eyed the pair, "I'm needed back at the office. Agent Shelly, you don't need to be told that you're lead on this one, and don't you dare tell me there's a serial killer among us."

Agents Treehorn and Shelly watched as she stomped away. Someone had delivered more bad news.

"How can another human being treat someone like this?" asked Samantha as she examined the homicide victim. The CSU team assisted her as they rolled out plastic to wrap the body in as they transferred the corpse to the body bag. Samantha was aware of Treehorn has he watched her every movement, as she was aware of his.

Agent Shelly asked, "Do you have a cause of death, Doc?"

"Strangulation, my guess. There's petechial hemorrhaging, as Trooper Allen reported. She's only been dead a few hours. I'll start the autopsy as soon as I get her back to the morgue." The doctor's phone beeped. She examined the text. "Darcy Clearwater's test results are back. The morgue faxed them to the FBI. The blood from the trash can matched Darcy's neck injury. These murders each have a different m.o."

"Thanks, Doc." Agent Shelly felt the tension between Treehorn and the doctor. "I'll go find something to do." Raven whistled the notes of the Pink Panther theme as he walked away.

Treehorn gave Raven a dirty look.

"I didn't proposition that woman for sex." Treehorn never once in his life explained his actions to a woman.

"Men do it, here, all the time."

"I don't, but it's what you thought when you overheard Buckman."

"This is not my first rodeo, Agent Treehorn. I'm broken, so you sought companionship elsewhere."

"It wasn't like that. I paid her for information. Donovan was getting back at both of us."

"Did he take it out on your face?"

"Lakken men told me that I wasn't welcome here. I disagreed. They're interfering in Darcy's investigation."

"I'm sorry. Did Bobby Beltram have a motive for her death?"

"He informed me she had problems with some of their employees and her advocacy with the MMIW. Shelly and I will work through the threats to see if anyone stands out."

"Her remaining forensics results should arrive soon, including the analysis of her Jeep."

"When are we going to talk about it?" Treehorn directed the conversation back to them.

"There is no 'it' to talk about," Samantha stressed, and turned and walked away, "Nice fat lip by the way." Damn it, she wanted to kiss it and comfort him.

The agent rubbed his swollen and sore face; it wasn't hard to conclude that fact. He watched the CSU team as they worked the crime scene. They meticulously removed and bagged the red dresses that hung from the tree limb. He stood stoically like generations of warriors before him, arms folded across his chest, and a pensive expression on his face.

Raven came up behind and said, "Women!"

"Shut up, Raven."

"I have to say it's nice, my friend, that you've taken an interest in a woman for more than just sex."

"Shut up, Raven."

His friend whispered, "She has a nice ass." He poked the wolf.

Treehorn turned to his friend this time and not to gently grabbed his friend's shoulder, same place, harder bruising intensity, and whispered fighting words, "If you say another word, I'm going to give you a lip just like mine."

Raven Shelly wasn't stupid, he knew his friend would do it, and he didn't want a matching fat lip. His wife liked his face just the way it was. He backed down, again.

Treehorn released his friend to walk away, "I'm paying my respects to Sandy's family."

Treehorn and a quiet Raven drove to Kaya Massey's house. The younger agent telephoned her with the news that her cousin Sandy had been found. It was never a pleasant duty for any law enforcement to deliver news of a death.

Kaya opened the door for them when they arrived at her little homestead. Their introductions were brief since a tea kettle whistled and prevented conversation.

The agents settled on the sofa while Kaya served them a hot drink.

"How did she die?" Kaya asked.

"It appears to be strangulation. The medical examiner has her body."

Kaya's hand shook, and a few drops of liquid splashed onto her crisp, clean Williston Cleaning Service uniform.

"I asked her here to help her get out of the prostitution." Kaya set aside her tea. "She promised she'd stop, but once she arrived, she stated the money was too good. It was the only thing she knew."

"We're sorry," Treehorn sympathized. He'd seen it over time, women caught in the vicious cycle, especially with prostitution.

"You know it was Lakken, right?" Kaya voiced her opinion.

"Why do you say that?" Treehorn asked.

"Who else could it be? Robert Beltram sits in his fancy house drinking his fancy red wine while his company rapes this land. He uses his money to control the community, and sometimes the law."

Treehorn understood what she was saying. "We have two dead Navajos. I know Sandy was only here a short time, but are there any details you've remembered since Agent Shelly interviewed you?"

Kaya shook her head, "None."

"Have any witnesses come forth and contacted you?" He grilled.

"No, Agent Treehorn, my phone hasn't rung once. Sandy arrived, and disappeared a week later. All of her johns were Lakken employees or related to its company. That's what I know, because that's what Sandy told me. Do you work for Lakken like other police officers?"

Treehorn took no offense. "I'll handcuff any man breaking the law."

Kaya responded, "I'd rather see him shot dead on the spot. That's how I feel when I see crime go unpunished in this town."

Treehorn removed a business card. "Do you need any help with the arrangements?"

"Bobby Beltram and the MMIW contacted me before you arrived. They offered to pay for Sandy's body to be returned to the reservation for burial."

"Agent Shelly and I will do our best to try to find who's responsible."

"Start with Robert Beltram. He's the root of all evil here."

Treehorn and Raven departed with heavy hearts.

"I'll check with the state police to see if they have any updated information," Raven offered.

Treehorn doubted they would have any. Whoever had held Sandy carried a sickness. No one tortures someone like that unless they have an evil inside them they can't remove.

Hell in Darkness

Janie knew this wasn't going to end well. It was hard to keep the panic away in the confinement of a room that was designed for sexual torture. The absolute silence unnerved her. She had regained consciousness as Brody dragged her into his prison and shackled her ankle. Janie survived the quick and brutal sexual assault. The girls in her line of work knew it was only a matter of time before they would cross paths with a john who was dangerous, it's not like normal men seek prostitutes; but how does one identify a killer in their midst? Janie didn't pray but hoped that if she made it through this; she would find a way to repay her savior.

Treehorn and Agent Shelly returned to the office to examine updates but as soon as they arrived, they felt the tension in the agency. The agent observed CSU Wilkerson in Buckman's office busy as she collected evidence bags.

Two older, serious suits stood at attention and observed the process. Someone screwed up.

Treehorn and Raven went to their office and focused on their investigations. They hoped the updated forensic and lab results of Darcy's would help. The steel shavings taken from her skin and the oil residue taken from the dress matched products used in the energy refinery business. No surprise there.

Raven had forwarded the crime photos of Sandy Begay to the office and the staff had printed them for him. He pinned them to the board. They weren't pretty.

"I sent the image of the red dress and its label to the dressmaker. They confirmed it was Darcy's. They had designed several dresses for her. The lab will go over it with a fine-tooth comb to see what else they can gather from it. Someone wrote, "Mommy" on it. The second red dress was labeled with a MMIW tag." Treehorn examined the image the CSU lab technician captured of the two red dresses swaying in the wind as if they were spirits calling out to them.

"The lab results confirmed the DNA on Darcy's dress belonged to Sandy. Can we assume they were killed by the same person?"

"No, but someone has to stop him or them." Treehorn slid his finger over the second red dress image. "Stolen Sisters, Raven; two dead Indians. How many more, when the MMIW count is over eighteen hundred?"

"I don't know, but even one is too many. Why would the killer dump Sandy's body at Darcy's body drop location?"

Treehorn examined the other crime scene photographs. The body was positioned at the base of the tree, inside the yellow police ribbon, with the tree and two red dresses in the background. If Treehorn didn't already know it was the exact crime scene he would have stated that it looked staged? "What else have we got?"

"The lab identified the bag had gingersnap cookie crumbs, and there was milk residue in the glass. Darcy's fingerprints weren't on my badge, only an unidentified print that matched the bag.

Treehorn examined the crime scene images of the note, badge, and plastic bag. Beneath those photos was the top half of the *Indian Times* newspaper.

Raven asked, "Serial killer?"

"A serial killer with two MOs?"

"The red dress and the body dump location. Those things connect the two cases, but we have two different CODs. Two killers?"

"Did someone place Sandy's body there to jerk us around since it was common knowledge that Darcy's body was dumped there?"

"True, but we have a third similarity."

"What's that?"

"They're both Navajo."

"Yes, they're both Indian." Raven watched Treehorn process the information from the bulletin board, "What are you thinking?"

"We need to re-examine these crimes from a different angle. I want you to cross reference the thousands of cases from the Missing and Murdered Indigenous Women with the major crimes database in the US."

"What am I looking for?"

"Murders and violent crimes that occurred within a hundred miles of Lakken Energy fields. Check the FBI database for every American Indian woman who was murdered or missing in the last twenty-five years. Cross reference them with the MMIW, locations, MO, and also see if prostitution was involved. Cross reference them with every Lakken Energy operation location."

"How will that help us find a killer?" Raven questioned.

"Cross reference current energy employees here to the same Lakken employees during the time frames when Indigenous women were murdered or disappeared. Cross reference Jasper Redmond's files. There may be updated information in there that's not in the system."

"You think the killer works for Lakken?"

"Yes. I hope it will allow us to narrow down a list to identify a killer. Start with the men here and include Brody Hauler. He's violent enough to have a history. Check with the Mental Health database, too."

"It'll take time, but I'll use due diligence."

"Do you need help?" Treehorn offered.

"I'll work on it during the evening when it's quieter here. It's what I prefer."

Treehorn admired his friend's work ethic.

Raven asked, "Why did the killer carve your name on Sandy?"

"He wanted my attention, and the killer is making this personal."

"Why?"

"Two possible reasons: to keep my eye on this case or to keep my eye away from something else."

"The killer or killers don't know your dedication."

"This is true."

Buckman appeared at the agents' office door and pointed at Treehorn, "I need to talk to you."

Treehorn followed Buckman to her office. The two other suits sat outside her door and examined their phones. They glanced at Treehorn as he passed, then ignored him. Buckman closed her door. She handed Treehorn a pair of latex gloves which he put on and gave him an envelope that was addressed to him. "I received an interesting box this morning filled with incriminating evidence and two letters. I've read mine."

Treehorn slit open his envelope:

Agent Treehorn,

Thank you for your help. I chose this life, it didn't choose me. I'm taking your advice. I contacted my sister in Fargo. I'm out of the business and plan on returning to college. I sent a letter to your boss letting them know that Agent Donovan was going to use me to set you up. Darcy Clearwater taught me Hooker 101. You'll soon understand.

Janie Marie Nettles

Treehorn angled the letter which allowed Buckman to read it and then he inserted it inside an evidence bag which was prepped.

Buckman closed her office blinds effectively blocking the staff's view into her office. She activated her DVD player for ten seconds. It showed Agent Donovan striking Janie. She shut it off in disgust.

Treehorn stood tall and his pursed lips were the only sign of his anger.

Buckman activated her speaker, "Denise, can you please have Agent Donovan report to my office."

"Yes, ma'am."

"I'm sorry," His temporary supervisor issued her apology.

Treehorn stood tall, silent, and angry; the only indication, his clenched fist.

"I want you to stay for this."

Agent Donovan knocked on the door.

"Come in." Buckman ordered.

Donovan entered and stopped when he saw Treehorn.

"Close the door, Agent Donovan." She pointed to a spot next to Treehorn and Donovan walked to it. She examined the two FBI agents in front of her. Both were dressed as the embodiment of the FBI. Crisp white shirts, conservative neckties, pressed pants, and shined shoes. Service weapons, badges, and handcuffs were neatly secured on their belts. Buckman recalled Leo Mancuso's conversation regarding his assignment of the half Navajo agent to her neck of the woods, "Treehorn won't disappoint you." Buckman felt a twinge of remorse. She read his impeccable service record and now felt she had disappointed him. She sensed her evening was going to be one hell of a migraine.

"Agent Donovan, please surrender your badge and service weapon."

"What!" The agent's face paled.

"Special Agent Treehorn, I'll give you the honor of handcuffing him."

Donovan demanded, "Why?"

"Janie Marie Nettles," Buckman stated.

"She's Treehorn's whore," Agent Donovan swore feebly in his weakened defense.

"I think not, Mr. Donovan. Surrender your service weapon and your badge or I'll have Treehorn remove them."

Donovan placed his weapon and holster on his supervisor's desk, then unclipped his badge from his belt. He rubbed his thumb over it for the last time and placed it on top of his weapon. They didn't ask, but Donovan removed his handcuffs and dropped them next to his weapon.

Treehorn picked up Donovan's cuffs, for there was no greater insult to a disgraced agent to be arrested and cuffed with his own pair. "Turn around!" Treehorn ordered.

Donovan didn't budge, so Treehorn moved to the dirty agent's back, grabbed Donovan's wrists, and cuffed him.

"Are you going to believe this half-breed over me?"

Treehorn grabbed the back of Donovan's head and smashed his face down onto his badge and service weapon, effectively fracturing his nose. Blood gushed down his face and dripped onto his crisp white shirt and tie.

"Resisting arrest is never a good option, ex-Agent Donovan," Buckman stated scornfully as she opened her door and motioned for the other two suits to enter her office.

Treehorn grabbed Donovan by the back of his shirt collar and squeezed the man's tie tighter. "You once asked me about my name. My father's John. He called me Treehorn so that I would never forget that I'm half Indian and to be proud of where I come from. He did it out of respect."

The suits made a timely entrance.

Buckman ordered, "He's all yours. Read him his rights, witness it, and document it."

Treehorn turned Donovan by the neck toward the men and shoved him hard.

"I want to press charges against Agent Treehorn. He broke my nose," whined Donovan.

"The ex-agent resisted arrest. Agent Treehorn had to subdue him. That's what both our reports will state."

Treehorn curled his lip in contempt as he stood silent.

"Mr. Donovan, these men are from Internal Affairs. When they're finished with you, they'll be turning you over to the DEA." Like a magician, Buckman conjured an evidence bag filled with hundred dollars bills. "You can explain to them how these serial-numbered bills that belonged to a DEA informant turned up with your fingerprints on them."

"The whore had them."

"If I had a dollar for every time someone from law enforcement told me that one!"

Buckman and Treehorn watched the Internal Affairs officers drag Donovan away in disgrace. Every staff member and agent in the office watched the fired officer's walk of shame.

The supervisor looked at Treehorn, "Have your statement on my desk within the hour."

Treehorn nodded once and walked out.

Chapter Eleven

Treehorn finished his paperwork quickly and efficiently. He inserted it into a labeled envelope and left it on Buckman's desk.

He returned to his office and examined the case bulletin board and the *Indian Times* newspaper picturing Raven, Samuel, and him that was enclosed in an evidence bag. He wondered why Darcy had left him a note.

He removed the tack that held the newspaper to the bulletin board and flipped it over to read the bottom half of the page. A reporter had written a story on the environmental protesters outside of Lakken Energy offices. Nothing out of the ordinary for the *Indian Times*. A company made money and the environment paid the price. At the bottom, a footnote read, "Lakken Sponsors Community Event, Page 2." Treehorn removed the paper from the evidence plastic and opened it to the next page. There stood Robert Beltram shooting a shotgun for a local pheasant hunting community event. A second image showed the CEO as he raised his glass in a toast upon receiving an award for the funding of clean water in developing areas. Treehorn refolded and reinserted the newspaper into the evidence bag and pinned it back on the bulletin board.

Raven opened a folder. "I examined Brenda Beltram's MVA from the Montana Highway Patrol. Straightforward, Nichelle Walters's intoxication level was twice the legal limit, she crossed the center line, and struck Beltram's vehicle head on. Mrs. Beltram died from the injuries. Mrs. Walters was arrested, jailed, and released after rehabilitation. Criminal charges were pending when she died. I pulled the investigative record of her death; incomplete in my opinion. The MHP found her in the car at the scene of the original MVA, dead. No sign of foul play, so they state, other than some bruises on her body that no one could account for. There were a few empty liquor bottles. The coroner ruled death by alcohol poisoning. We'll see what Dr. Reynolds concludes off the medical records."

Raven handed Treehorn the CSU lab results from Darcy's Jeep and its GPS history, "Notice anything interesting?"

Treehorn read them. "Yes, I do."

Raven asked, "Do you think the testing got her killed?"

"I don't know if it's a strong enough motive to kill," Treehorn answered. "I want you to pull the environmental reports Lakken submitted to Washington."

"I'll have them for you in the morning."

Treehorn handed Raven a sticky note. "Have them examined for this and keep it between us, not even the staff here."

Raven examined the yellow square, the same type Darcy had on her corpse with his badge, "I understand."

"I'll call the younger Beltram and see if he's willing to provide us with the information."

The CEO's son answered his phone on the first ring. "Beltram."

"John Treehorn."

"What can I do for you?"

"Can you repeat Darcy's movement on the day she died?"

"Sure. Darcy was in the office from eight to noon, then she drove out to Granite Ridge to obtain water samples, Agent Treehorn."

"Why water samples?" Treehorn inquired, though he thought he knew the answer.

"She was tracking a swarm of earthquakes in the area and she was curious as to why they'd occurred. She had several of our wells monitored in that location to try to determine if there was a correlation."

"And, when did she finish?" Treehorn asked even though he had her GPS map tracking her vehicle.

"I don't know if she returned to the office, but I know she clocked out with her assistant at 3 pm. We had dinner in town and returned to her apartment. I rode with her to the MMIW dinner. I caught a ride with an employee from there when the well blew out, so I don't know where she went after the ceremony."

"I'd like to thank you for covering Sandy Begay's funeral expenses."

"It's the least I can do, Agent Treehorn, especially since we both suspect it was a Lakken employee who killed her. We've caused enough problems in this community."

"Thanks for your time and the employee data. I forgot to ask, are you an only child?"

"Yes, I am. Why do you need to know?"

"I question all family members in an investigation. I'll keep you posted."

"Thank you."

Robert Beltram closed his office door and telephoned Brody Hauler.

"Agent Treehorn just questioned Bobby about Granite Ridge. Tail him, tell the men to keep him busy, and you know what to do to make it look like an accident."

The two agents drove to the morgue in their FBI frames of mind.

Raven's phone rang as the men walked the parking lot. "I'll catch up with you. It's Dana."

Treehorn's time had arrived to poke Raven. "Tell your wife you were admiring another woman's ass!"

Raven's eyes widened. "Treehorn said 'Hi.'"

Treehorn laughed. He knew who wore the pants in that household.

Raven countered, "You know Treehorn. He works me hard."

Treehorn chuckled as he walked away.

Juan buffed the floors as Treehorn walked the morgue's hallway with his long stride. The old man blocked Treehorn's progression.

"I'm here on official business." Treehorn stated to the janitor-cum-guard.

"Uh huh!"

"You can ask Dr. Reynolds."

Juan took one step back while he kept his eyes on Treehorn, "Hey, Doc! You want to see the G-man?"

Samantha wasn't slow on the uptake, "Which one, the pissant or *the John?*"

Treehorn opened his jacket and showed Juan his service weapon.

The janitor answered, "The smarter one."

Treehorn's lips quirked up as he passed the janitor.

Juan whispered, "Be good to her."

Treehorn nodded.

Samantha covered Sandy Begay's body with a sheet as Treehorn entered the morgue, "Where's Agent Shelly?"

"Speaking with his wife."

Samantha removed her gloves and washed her hands. "Would you like a cup of coffee? It's a fresh pot."

Treehorn's stomach heaved a little from the smell of the room. "I'll pass, but thanks for the offer."

Both ignored the elephant in the room as Samantha poured her coffee into her personalized mug, '*My other job's signing death certificates!*'

"Samantha…"

"Treehorn…"

Raven's untimely entrance made Treehorn grind his teeth.

Samantha watched as Treehorn and Raven stood respectfully next to the body as they waited for her report, "Sandy Begay. Age twenty-six. Cause of death, suffocation by strangulation. She was sexually assaulted and sodomized. I sent samples out for DNA testing. She wasn't washed. I've pulled trace epithelial cells from the nails and body, and trace evidence from her hair from the location where she was kept. Your name was carved post mortem."

Treehorn and Raven listened without commenting.

"The dress hung from the tree was positively identified as Darcy Clearwater's and it was the clothing she wore when she was murdered. I removed blood samples from it, including the blood spot from her neck laceration. I've sent everything to the labs. Someone wrote "Mommy" with a marker. The second dress hung from the tree was placed there by the MMIW."

Treehorn and Raven waited for the report's conclusion.

"She was beaten and raped repeatedly. The bruises cover her from head to toe and were administered over several days." Samantha voiced her anger, "How can anyone treat another human being like this?"

"What's your theory as a forensic ME?" Treehorn asked, but he knew this man was sick.

"My theory? Your killer was severely abused as a child, sexually abused, and beaten would be my opinion. You have a psychopathic killer on your hands. This man's killed before. He has demons that are chasing him to hell and back."

Raven asked, "Did he kill Darcy Clearwater?"

"I can't answer that, and neither can the evidence, yet. All I can tell you is that there were two different causes of death and the red dresses are the only evidence that join the cases. I'm not short on specimens. You either have one killer who has two MOs or two killers who may know each other."

"One or two killers…" Raven started.

"…doesn't matter how many. They need to be stopped," Treehorn finished.

"Did you know that Darcy's expensive watch had GPS? I requested its record be forwarded to your office."

Raven told Treehorn, "I'll look for it."

"We have a witness." Samantha flushed when Treehorn focused on her, "Remember the fingerprints on the drinking glass in Darcy's apartment and the fingerprints that matched the bag that held Agent Shelly's badge?" Both agents waited. "I tested the saliva from both glasses. The milk glass sample's a genetic match for a male from the Cheyenne River Lakota Nation and the fingerprints on the bag and rear door weren't partials, they are a boys. The same kid who took your badge, Agent Shelly."

Raven finally comprehended the events, "Why that little sh…"

"…thief." Treehorn interrupted, "We'll speak to him when he gets home from school."

"Remember I had the semen from Darcy's body retested after a discrepancy?" Samantha pulled the results and handed them to Treehorn. "One sample matched Bobby Beltram; the other is a familial match, a half-brother. He definitely touched the body after her death."

"Paternal or maternal parent?" Treehorn questioned.

"Most investigators wouldn't question that, but in this case, it's paternal. Robert Beltram fathered a second son."

Treehorn met Raven's eyes. "Bobby denied having a sibling."

"Did he know, or did he lie?" Raven asked.

189

"Or did Robert Beltram have no knowledge of fathering another child?" the doctor questioned.

"Let's keep this between the three of us. That man is either the killer or an accomplice, but either way, he knows who killed Darcy Clearwater." Treehorn moved his head at Raven who worked with his fellow agent long enough and understood the unspoken message, *"Investigate Robert Beltram's history."*

"What did you find on Brenda Beltram's autopsy?" Raven asked.

Samantha opened a file, "Cause of death. MVA. Nichelle Walters's car struck her vehicle head on. Mrs. Beltram died en route to the trauma unit from injuries she sustained in the accident. There were no drugs or alcohol in her system. She was returning to Williston after visiting friends. No foul play." Samantha handed the agents a photo of Brenda Beltram. She was a beautiful redhead with smiling blue eyes.

Treehorn returned the image to Samantha, "And Nichelle Walters?"

"This one's different. Mrs. Walters had a history of active alcoholism from a young age up until the day of the Beltram MVA. Her longest stretch of sobriety started the day after she killed Mrs. Beltram to the day she was found in her parked vehicle at the scene of the deadly accident. I found bruises and contusions that were inconsistent with someone who drove to a location and drank themselves to death. She suffered from asthma and carried an inhaler. The coroner ruled the cause of death was a combination of alcohol poisoning and an asthma attack."

"Did the coroner think she was *just* a drunken Indian?" Treehorn's fist clenched.

Samantha respected Treehorn's intuition. "I think you should re-interview the family." The ME handed Treehorn a document. "I'll need the family's permission to exhume the body for a re-examination."

"Why?" Raven asked.

"The most interesting statement was made by her daughter and documented: 'My mother only drank vodka, she was a selective alcoholic.'"

"What did the lab find in her body?" Treehorn asked.

"Scotch."

Treehorn caught Raven's eye and nodded toward the door.

"Thanks, Dr. Reynolds. I'll go re-examine…the police reports." Raven whistled *"Help"* by the Beatles as he walked away.

Samantha tried not to laugh but failed. "Where are the police reports?"

Treehorn cracked a smile. "Back at the office. People find it hard to believe he excels at criminal research." He stared into her green eyes and took a chance, "Would you like to have dinner tonight?"

"Yes." Samantha didn't hesitate.

"Six?"

Samantha nodded, "I'll call if I'm held up."

"Job comes first." Treehorn whistled *"Stranger"* by Billy Joel as he walked away.

Brody followed Treehorn's vehicle from the morgue to the Painted Pony Diner. He watched and rubbed his aching jaw as the agents purchased their take out and observed the agent interact with Cookie Lighthouse. He followed the men to their FBI offices and watched as he dropped off his co-worker.

Treehorn left Raven with instructions, "I'm going to drive out to Granite Ridge and look around. Check for the results from Washington and the LEOs documentation from Lakken sites. I should be back in an hour."

"Will do."

The road was busy with energy-related trucks moving equipment, pipe, and water but traffic lessened as Treehorn neared Granite Ridge. He removed his laboratory kit from the vehicle and walked around the area. In the distance, there was a network of perimeter roads to each oil well which were surrounded by outcroppings of granite and hardened ground. Treehorn had sent an email to Bobby Beltram for permission to obtain the water samples. He filled several containers where the water leached from the rocks and aquifer. It appeared to Treehorn that Mother Earth was crying.

Brody watched Treehorn through his rifle scope but lost sight of him when he disappeared behind a knoll. He returned the rifle to his truck when his co-workers' maintenance trucks arrived to work on the nearest well.

Brody called his dispatch, "Give me the location of our water trucks driving to Granite Ridge." He made several more calls as Treehorn packed his equipment into his vehicle and watched as he drove towards town.

Treehorn couldn't have foreseen Brody's plan when the Lakken Energy truck appeared in his lane and forced him off the road and into the ditch. The melted snow and slush mixed with the mud prevented the SUV's tires from gripping and allowing its return to the pavement.

Several Lakken trucks sped by as Treehorn inspected his vehicle for damage. Each driver made sure to honk and give the FBI agent the finger as they continued on their way.

The agent knew they wouldn't stop to assist him.

Brody telephoned Robert Beltram. "Treehorn took water samples from Granite Ridge."

"Where is he now?" Beltram demanded.

"In a ditch for a little while," Brody chuckled.

Beltram slammed down the telephone receiver in his office as the computer geek knocked on his door frame.

"We're in," Howie told his red-faced employer.

"It's about time, considering what I'm paying you," Beltram stated.

"Darcy added encryption protection on her computer. She wanted someone blocked."

"Obviously."

"Do you want the personal stuff, her wedding pictures?"

"No. I want the engineering files."

"You know her husband…"

"Damn it. I want the company files. I don't give a shit about anything else."

The computer geek's fingers sped across the keyboard. "She deleted a large file, but before she did, she emailed it to her phone. Let me see if I can recover it."

"Anything you recover, delete it permanently."

"I can't delete the file on her phone, only from your server."

"Have you dialed her phone?"

"Repeatedly. There's no response from it or its GPS. The battery hasn't been reinserted."

"Son of a bitch."

Beltram telephoned Brody. "We need to find Darcy's phone. Lucky for us the device was password protected."

"You own it right?" Brody asked.

"It's Lakken's property and the Feds can't access it without a subpoena," Beltram said.

Brody asked, "So, why are you worried? Unless the Feds have the phone and its password, they'll never access it."

"Where's Agent Asshole now?" Beltram asked.

"Still in the ditch." Brody watched the agent through his binoculars.

"Keep me posted," Beltram ordered as he slammed down the phone again.

North Dakota State Trooper Maresca turned on his red lights and stopped to assist the government issued vehicle in the ditch. When he identified the driver he asked, "I thought you Feds had your act together."

"I thought so too, but when a Lakken truck started playing chicken my options became limited."

The trooper put his hand out to the agent, "Alfred Maresca. Soon to be a Fed with the Marshal Service."

"John Treehorn, current Fed at FBI." He shook the offered hand.

"Did you catch their plate number?"

"I'll download the video when I return to the garage."

Treehorn connected the tow rope to his SUV connection and the trooper did likewise. A snug tug and the vehicle returned to the pavement from the muddy ditch.

The men removed the connected tow rope.

"What area do you want to focus on in the Marshal Service?" Treehorn asked as he returned the tow rope to his vehicle.

"I'm hoping prisoner transport since I'm a trained pilot, but I'll serve and protect wherever they assign me."

Treehorn handed the trooper his card. "If you ever need anything from the FBI, give me a call."

"Do you want me to follow you back to town to make sure the vehicle's safe?"

"I'd appreciate that."

Trooper Maresca kept his red lights on right to the FBI garage. His LEO humor wasn't lost on the agent.

When Treehorn arrived at the garage, he downloaded the video of the water truck as it swerved into his traffic lane and sent him into the ditch. Luck was on his side. His camera recorded the man's image and his license plate. He'd pay him a visit with a couple troopers before he left town.

After ordering a replacement vehicle, Treehorn went in search of the FBI lab with his several labeled and boxed water containers.

A staff member with the name tag "Dorris" greeted him, "Hello. New guy?"

The Navajo nodded once. "Agent John Treehorn. I'm here working a case."

"No one here works just *a case*."

Treehorn didn't disagree. "I have water samples for deposit."

"Let me call Anita and she'll take them from you. Here's the log for you to sign, since you're new in town." Treehorn complied with their regulations.

Another hard-working lab tech appeared. Anita handed Treehorn a lab slip attached to a clipboard. "What are we testing for?"

"Groundwater contaminates, the illegal variety," Treehorn answered as he filled in the form and placed the samples in a waiting box.

"I'll do the full spectrum. When do you need them?"

Treehorn smiled as he returned the clipboard.

Anita understood. "I'll get right on them."

"Thanks. Here's my card. If I'm not in the office could you please email me the results?"

Anita and Dorris nodded.

"Thanks."

"Good luck with that 'one case,'" Dorris reiterated.

As the tall, handsome agent walked away, the two techs looked at each other, and Anita asked, "One case?"

They laughed.

Meanwhile, Brody waited for the federal agent to reappear. He needed a plan to end this investigation.

Chapter Twelve

Brody followed Treehorn and another agent as they departed the FBI office and drove toward the town's center. Brody allowed a few vehicles to get between him and Fed as he trailed him from a distance. An ambulance and trooper forced him to pull over as they passed. Brody looked away as the lights of both vehicles passed him. He didn't need his childhood nightmares to intrude at this time.

The agents arrived at the Painted Pony Diner. Raven entered the front door and walked up to the boy as he unloaded cookies from a tray. "Hey, Paco, I wonder if your fingerprints on these cookies bags will match the print from my badge."

Paco slammed the tray into Raven's stomach forcing the agent to grab it, and the quick-thinking con artist ran towards the rear exit. The boy shot out the door where FBI Special Agent John Treehorn stood waiting with his handcuffs swinging.

The kid tried to dodge around him, but the agent grabbed the kid by the waist. "Where do you think you're going?"

"Let me go!" The kid's legs flailed in the wind.

Raven arrived. "I'll use my handcuffs. I have kid's size."

"I didn't kill her." the kid cried.

"We know, Paco." Treehorn said.

"You do?" The boy stopped his struggle.

Treehorn stood him on the ground still swinging his handcuffs. "Don't even think of running," he stated firmly.

Paco looked at the alley and its traffic, "Can we go back inside?"

Treehorn nodded toward the door as he put away his handcuffs.

Raven hid the smile behind a fake cough as his partner won over the kid.

Brody found the agent's vehicle parked at the diner and maneuvered his truck, so he could see one of the agents through the front window. He lacked a direct line of sight to Treehorn but knew the agents were together. He didn't see the boy hidden from his view sitting in the booth.

The agents and the boy sat in a secluded seating away from the ears of other customers. The waitress delivered coffee for the Feds and milk for the boy.

"You're not in any trouble." Treehorn put the boy's fears to rest.

Paco looked at Raven and his badge on his belt.

"You're not in trouble for taking my badge," Raven stated.

"What did you see?" Treehorn asked as Raven pulled out his notepad.

Paco removed his cookies from his pocket. He offered the crushed cookies to each agent, who shook their heads. "I was walking home from the diner when Darcy saw me. She stopped and asked if I wanted a ride home. I told her my momma wouldn't be home from the diner for a couple of hours and daddy was working the fields, so Darcy invited me over to her place. She didn't want me going home alone and I've been to her house before. She called and left a message with my mother and let her know I was safe."

"Go on," Treehorn encouraged, "tell us the whole story."

"She gave me milk and cookies as I watched a movie. Darcy called someone and whispered happy things to them.

202

She made funny kissing sounds that made us both laugh. Someone called her and upset her. Darcy went to her desk and did some stuff. I was bored so I turned off the TV and went to see what she was doing. She pointed to the *Indian Times* newspaper and said, 'Those are the men you should look up to.' Your picture was on the cover. We saw headlights in the window and this upset her. She wrote '*Call FBI Agent John Treehorn*' on a yellow note. Darcy put the note on her phone inside my cookie bag and told me to hide under the bed. Someone pounded on the door. I ran and hid. I saw his brown shoes. He screamed at her about some file. She quit her job; yelled something about a crime. I think he hit her because she fell and hit the garbage can. I was so scared because she looked at me and didn't move. I saw a brown shoe stomp on her hand and I saw a man's hand reach down and take off her ring." Tears ran down Paco's face. "He said no one misses you, but I miss her."

Treehorn handed the kid a few napkins to wipe his face. "Go on."

Raven gave the kid a nod of encouragement.

"The shoes walked around the bed to the bathroom. He called someone and told them that he had a body. I grabbed my coat and ran out the back door with the note. I hid down the block."

"What happened next?" Treehorn handed the kid a couple more napkins.

"I saw a guy driving a red truck. He works for Lakken. I've seen him around. He's real mean. He went into Darcy's apartment and I got into the back of his truck and hid in his tool box. The mean guy comes out carrying Darcy and put her into the back of the truck and covered her. I was really scared."

"You were very brave."

Paco tried to smile. "The man told the other man he wanted her washed before he dumped her. He ordered her dress washed. I didn't see that man's face, only the mean one. I stayed in the tool box while he drove out of town. It wasn't far, a few miles to his house. He took Darcy inside. I was really scared. I didn't know where I was. I thought I heard screaming. My phone didn't work out there so all I could do was to wait."

"I'm really proud of you, and your mother will be, too," Treehorn added.

Paco smiled. "I've tried to be good, so my momma doesn't have to worry about me. She works hard."

"Keep it up," Treehorn stated.

Paco finished his crumbs. "He came back to the truck carrying Darcy. She had on a different red dress. He drove back to town and out to the old oak tree next to the highway sign. He dumped her in the snow and drove back to town. When he stopped at the light, I jumped out and ran into a crowd." Paco looked nervous.

"What happened next?" Treehorn focused on the kid.

"Darcy's phone rang. The man searched for me in the crowd to find it. He started to swear, and he yelled, 'Winston, catch that kid!' I didn't look back but ran through the people and hid. I opened the bag and answered the phone. The same man's voice who hurt Darcy spoke on the phone, 'I'm going to find you and kill you.' I hung up and I took out the battery."

"What did you do after that?" Treehorn asked.

"I hid until I knew the man had stopped looking for me. I ran to the diner to tell my momma. When I got there I saw him." Paco pointed toward Agent Shelly. "I saw his badge and knew he was searching for a missing lady."

"Why didn't you tell me?" Raven asked.

"The man standing next to you wore the same brown shoes that hurt Darcy." Treehorn eyed Raven and his face asked, *"Do you remember who?"*

Raven shook his head.

"What did you do next, Paco?" Treehorn questioned.

"I was walking out when I saw his badge, so I took it. I put it in the bag with Darcy's note. I rode my bike out to Darcy and left the badge and note in her hand. It snowed so I knew no one would know I was there. I came back to town and scratched Trooper Allen's car with MM 224. It's his patrol area. He's a good cop. He'd work it out. If he didn't, I would have found another way to get the police. I knew the badge with the note would get help from the important police. I saw it on TV."

"We're on the case now, Paco. That's what's important," Treehorn said.

"I should have talked to you," Paco looked to the younger agent. "I'm sorry I took your badge. I thought you were bad, like that Donovan guy."

"It's OK." Raven smiled.

"I should have believed you. Darcy showed me your picture on the *Indian Times*." Paco offered in tune with his apology. "I knew Trooper Allen found Darcy when I saw the other police go down the road with their lights and sirens."

"We're proud of you for helping a victim." Treehorn opened his palm in front of Paco.

The boy understood. He dug into his pants pocket and removed an expensive phone and its separated battery, both enclosed in a plastic bag. "If you put the battery in, the bad men will find you."

"No, Paco, it's the other way around. We'll find them." Treehorn stood and let the boy out of their booth. He removed a business card and placed it into the boy's pocket. "One day, I hope you choose the FBI academy. You would do us proud."

Paco smiled and ran out the back door as Treehorn pocketed Darcy's phone.

"Starting them young?" Raven asked.

"I got you, didn't I?" Treehorn smiled.

Raven shined his badge, "Yes, you did, and I've been grateful ever since."

Brody watched from his red truck as the two agents paid and walked out of the diner carrying coffees at the same time Dr. Reynolds drove into the parking lot. He watched as they exchanged a brief conversation. Then, he observed Treehorn as he leaned close to the woman and whispered in her ear. The woman smiled, nodded, and went into the diner while the Fed and his co-worker climbed into their vehicle and drove away.

"Screw you, Agent Prick; I know what will bring you to your knees."

Brody thought of his plan of action as he waited and watched for the medical examiner.

Samantha purchased her coffee and walked to her car.

Brody wondered why she sat in her car, unmoving. Then, he saw her holding her telephone.

Samantha took a deep breath, dialed Bobby Beltram's number, and felt a slight relief when her call went to his voicemail. "Bobby Beltram, this is Dr. Samantha Reynolds. I have a copy of Darcy's death certificate. Can you please call me? I have something important to discuss with you before I release the document." Samantha dreaded the wait until he returned her call because she didn't know how he would react when she informed him of his wife's pregnancy. If the medical examiner hadn't been focused on her job and Treehorn, she may have noticed the red truck that followed her to the FBI housing.

Brody trailed the doctor at a safe distance which prevented her from noticing him. He watched as she parked, gathered her belongings, and unlocked her door. He backed his vehicle into the parking slot so his driver's side was next to hers, then made a call to his employee with firm instructions. He tuned his CB to the police channel and waited.

"911 Dispatch. Attention all LEOs in the vicinity of Spring Lake Park and Route 2. There's a report of a vehicle and pedestrian accident with fatality. Nearest trooper please report your availability and ETA. Medical examiner Reynolds has been notified."

Brody turned off the radio and grabbed his "Tag & Bag." A handy little kit he put together that contained plastic ties, duct tape, and his trusted stun gun.

Samantha secured her room in a hurry and focused on calling Treehorn. She didn't notice the man sitting in his truck. She unlocked her car door and opened it when she heard the stun gun activate and the pain radiated into her hip. She couldn't support her weight and sprawled into her front seat. Her purse, keys, and cell phone dropped to the floor. The stun gun was pressed into her back and the arc was activated for a few more seconds. Her lungs contracted painfully into a full-blown panic attack and she lost consciousness.

Brody examined the parking lot, dragged Samantha out of her car and placed her into his truck cab. He closed her car door, then climbed into his truck. He played with his telephone, so he wouldn't draw attention to himself as a stranger exited the parking lot. He pushed Samantha down onto the passenger side floor and covered her with an old tarp from behind his seat. The voices in his head whispered their mantra: *"He'll figure it out. He'll figure it out."* Brody drove out of the parking lot and detoured past the FBI office where he observed Treehorn's parked vehicle. He smiled and leisurely traveled home to his man cave.

Treehorn read the lab report from Washington that had arrived while he was out. He handed it to Raven. Treehorn checked the mandatory boxes on his computer for a search warrant, printed it, and handed it to his co-worker. "Have a judge sign this and execute it immediately."

"What are we looking for?" Raven found the answer as he examined the paper.

"The two items the killer had in his possession after killing Darcy. Take one agent and one lab tech. Quiet, in and out," Treehorn ordered. "And, Raven, document everything."

The agent nodded and departed to execute the search.

Treehorn stood and examined the bulletin board of women. Grandmothers, aunts, daughters, sisters, cousins, nieces, and mothers, all had their time ended by foul play.

He looked at the expensive watch his father had given him the day he graduated from the FBI academy. It was nearing the time of his scheduled meeting as he walked to a communications room in the building.

Doug Ryan, media technician, waited for him in the sound booth. "Agent Treehorn?"

The agent nodded, "Is she ready?"

The television screen showed a professionally-dressed Indian woman in her late 30s who was waiting patiently while a technician wired her with a microphone. Behind her, a large window opened to the spacious prairie in her backyard.

"Have a seat and I'll adjust the picture and sound. Then, you'll be good to go." Doug closed his booth and Treehorn heard a couple of beeps, and the sound guy gave the agent the thumbs up.

"Norma Baker?" Treehorn asked.

The woman nodded.

"FBI Special Agent John Treehorn. Thank you for speaking to me today. I'm sorry for not having the time to drive to Fort Peck for this interview."

"That's fine. At least someone is asking me about my mother."

"Tell me about Nichelle Walters."

"You mean the mother who was never there?" Norma asked bitterly.

"The story you want to tell." Treehorn prompted.

"My mother was an alcoholic from the time she could obtain liquor. If she couldn't afford it, then she used her body in exchange for it."

"Go on."

"I moved out when I turned sixteen because I couldn't take it anymore. The short periods of sobriety were eclipsed by longer periods of her being a drunk."

"What happened the day of the motor vehicle accident?" Treehorn questioned.

"No one knows how she got her hands on a set of keys. One of my brothers or sisters left them on the table. The next thing they knew she drove off to find liquor."

"What happened?"

"The collision occurred twenty miles east of here. It was nighttime and raining. My mother visited her sister near Williston, bought some alcohol, and drove back here to Fort Peck. She drove drunk and plowed head-on into Brenda Beltram's car."

"What happened next?" Treehorn wrote on his pad.

Norma looked away and found a Kleenex. "The hospital cleared her medically for the car accident and she detoxed in jail. A judge sentenced her to supervised rehabilitation."

"How long was she in treatment?"

"Six months. Her criminal charges remained pending after they discharged her, and she finally found the one thing she couldn't hold onto before the accident, her sobriety. I guess killing an innocent person affects some drunks more so than others."

"Are you saying she was sober, up until the day she died?"

"Yes."

"Tell me about that day." Treehorn requested.

"She came over for breakfast. We visited, drank coffee. She offered to cook dinner. I gave her money for the groceries and she planned on returning to use my kitchen." Norma's voice broke and she used tissues to wipe her tears.

Treehorn waited while she composed herself.

"The state police found her body inside her car in the ditch at the same location as the Beltram collision. The *exact* location."

"I've read the police report and coroner's review. What do you think is missing?" the agent asked.

"The truth? Did they document that I demanded a second autopsy? Did they note that I disagreed with their findings?" Norma voiced her anger.

"Please explain."

"First of all, my mother didn't remember where the accident occurred. The jail staff posted pictures of the two twisted vehicles outside her jail cell, so she would see them twenty-four seven what she had done. During her eight months of sobriety, Agent Treehorn, not once did my mother go within twenty miles of that accident site. She refused, point blank, to drive or even ride along that stretch of highway. She detoured around it, regardless of how many miles it added or how much longer it took."

"What else?"

"My mother religiously wore the underwear the jail had issued her with her name tagged in them for their laundry. She never wanted to forget her jail time."

"A sad but admirable tradition." Treehorn stated.

"Her underwear wasn't with her at the autopsy."

The agent made a note of that information. "What else?"

"She had all of the grocery money I gave her still in her pocket, unspent. The police reported that she died of alcohol poisoning. How did she get the booze? I demanded her death be ruled a homicide."

"Why?"

"The alcohol that was found in my mother's body wasn't what she drank."

"Why's that a crime?"

"My mother never drank Scotch."

"Alcoholics drink what they can get their hands on."

"That's where you're wrong, Agent Treehorn. My mother was allergic to Scotch, or more precisely, to barley. Any amount would make her go into anaphylactic shock, her throat would close up and she would die of asphyxiation. She carried an EpiPen in her purse. It wasn't used."

"The coroner ruled the death accidental."

"I read the death certificate. Accidental death by alcohol poisoning! She was just another dead Indian no one cared about."

"The forensic medical examiner here wants to re-examine your mother. We need your permission to exhume her body."

"My mother's body was cremated and her ashes given to the wind."

Treehorn watched behind Norma as a red dress hung from the tree limb moved as if its spirit danced for him. There would be no answers in Nichelle Walter's death today.

Treehorn returned to his office and wrote Nichelle Walter's date of death on her image. He looked at the women on the board again and knew he didn't have the clue that connected these women's deaths.

Chapter Thirteen

His desk phone speaker activated. "Agent Treehorn, call on line 3."

"Agent Treehorn."

"Hi. This is Carol Johnson, Janie Nettle's sister."

"How can I help you?" he asked.

"Well, Janie called me last night and told me she would be on the shuttle bus today from Williston. I went to pick her up, but she wasn't there. Janie gave me your number to call in case of an emergency."

"Is that the last shuttle of the day?"

"Yes, that's why I'm calling."

"Can I have your number and Janie's?" Treehorn wrote on his pad. "I'll make some inquiries here on this end," he offered. "If she contacts you, can you give me a call? If I locate her, I'll call you."

Carol agreed. "Thank you."

Treehorn hung up the telephone and walked directly to central holding, the door was opened so he didn't have to present his identification. "Is Dennis Donovan still here?"

An older gentleman, Weldon, sat quietly behind a no-nonsense desk. "Why, do you want to go another round with him?"

Clearly the gossip mill worked in this small office. "Is he still here?"

"Yes. His transport paperwork somehow got screwed up, so he's here until morning." Weldon pointed to his right. "He's at the end. Just don't kill him. I don't want the paperwork."

Treehorn didn't joke. "I promise he'll be alive when I leave him."

Dennis Donovan looked worse for wear; his face was swollen and bruised from the nose-badge incident. He was reading some obscure book on warfare on the water. Treehorn never took him for a Navy guy. Pickings must have been slim for jailhouse readers.

"What do you know about Janie Marie Nettles?"

Donovan ignored Treehorn, then he realized that might not be in his best interests. "What's there to know? She wasn't that memorable in the sack." He knew that would get a rise out of the self-righteous prick.

Treehorn didn't react, he just stared.

Donovan felt the sweat beneath his shirt. "Kind of hard for me to know anything while I'm in a cell without a cell."

Treehorn watched for a reaction from the corrupt ex-agent. "She didn't arrive at her destination today."

"This helps my case, right?" asked the dirty agent with an agenda.

"Not if you arranged foul play."

Donovan laughed, "You come to this town and think you know everything in a few days." He chuckled. "The whoring, drugs, and crime? You're just scraping the scum off the top of the barrel, Mr. Treehorn. You have no clue what transpires here."

"I'm not in jail." The interrogation was done so he turned and walked away.

"You know what's great about being in jail…" Donovan shouted at Treehorn's retreating back, "…it's the perfect alibi."

The Special Agent knew that to be true.

Treehorn returned to his office desk as his phone pinged with a message from Raven, *"Mission accomplished."*

The agent texted a handcuff symbol.

He unlocked his desk drawer and removed Darcy's telephone and inserted the battery to power it up. The phone's password screen appeared. Treehorn messaged Bobby Beltram from his own cell phone, *"I've located Darcy's phone. What's her password?"*

Bobby Beltram replied a minute later, *"0815"*

Treehorn typed in 0-8-1-5 and a secondary password screen appeared with seven lines. He typed in B-E-L-T-R-A-M and the screen stated "Wrong—1 try remains."

He messaged Bobby again, "What's her second password?"

A ping returned after a few seconds. *"She only had one password."*

Treehorn powered down the phone, returned it to its evidence bag inside his drawer, and locked it securely.

Robert Beltram's in-house telephone buzzed. "What?"

Howie, the computer nerd, replied, "Someone activated Darcy Clearwater's telephone's GPS."

"What's its location?" the CEO demanded.

"The FBI office," the kid answered.

"Can you access the phone and delete the file?"

"No."

"Why the hell not?"

"The phone powered down again."

Beltram reached for his glass of Scotch.

"Have you broken the password on the laptop?"

"Still working on it."

"Stop talking and get back to work." the CEO
ordered before downing the drink.

Robert Beltram phoned Brody in his truck, "Where's
Treehorn?"

"At his office," Brody answered.

"Someone's activated Darcy's cell phone."

"Have your lawyers get on it," Brody demanded.
"You're always bitching about how much they cost."

"Let me know when he leaves." Beltram said.

"I have a delivery to make. I don't have time to
babysit him all day." Brody glanced at his speedometer as
he drove past the speed limit sign. He didn't need any
attention on him right now. His passenger moaned.

"You do what I tell you to do."

"Trust me when I say that prick will be running
around in circles in a couple of hours. Don't worry about
him."

Beltram knew Treehorn had something on him, but nothing that was important. He'd trust Brody to keep the Fed busy.

"Stay out of trouble," Beltram ordered.

"Yes, boss," Brody answered as he drove across the bridge to his property.

Raven arrived as Treehorn hung up his telephone. "I delivered the two items to the lab for testing. We were in and out with no problem."

"Good job. While you were gone, I received a call from Janie Nettles' sister in Fargo. Janie didn't arrive on the shuttle as planned. I called Thirsty's Bar and they haven't seen her today."

"We know she mailed a package from the post office to here," Raven powered up his computer.

"You take the post office, I'll take the shuttle. Let's see if we can find her."

The agents loaded Janie's arrest image into their computers and focused on their work, before her photo became another statistic on the MMIW bulletin board.

Janie huddled in the corner on a filthy pad and tried to squeeze warmth out of a threadbare blanket. She didn't move when her jailer open the door.

Brody dropped a semi-conscious woman next to her. "I brought you some company."

Janie doubted that.

Brody's crazy eyes traced the outline of Samantha's body in her medical examiners clothing. "I'll be back with a present for her and beer for me. We're going to celebrate."

Janie doubted that, too!

She waited until Brody locked the door before she approached the other woman.

Janie shook her. "Hey, are you hurt?"

Samantha tried to focus on the woman's voice as she regained consciousness from her nightmare. Her hand touched the dirty floor beneath her instead of her cotton covered bed. "Where am I?"

"I would guess Brody Hauler's man cave. Did you want me to be honest or lie?"

"I can't decide. I'm Samantha."

"Janie."

"How did you come to be here?"

"I was on my way to the bus shuttle to take me away from here. Brody offered me a late-night lift, a knockout punch, and here I am. You?"

"Medical Examiner. A reported death made me rush to my car. I didn't see him, but I felt his stun gun. I had a panic attack and blacked out. Do you know him?"

"Brody Hauler. Mean SOB. He works for Lakken. Girls in my profession avoided him for just cause."

Samantha examined Janie's face by the single light bulb. "How's the jaw?"

Janie rubbed it. "It's sore as hell. I should have left this town a few days ago when I had the chance."

"Why didn't you?"

"I made plans to bring down a dirty FBI Agent and I hoped it worked."

"Dennis Donovan?"

"How'd you know?"

"Small town, and it worked."

"Can we huddle for warmth? I can't seem to get warm." Janie asked.

Samantha placed her arms around Janie. "Do you have any other injuries?"

Janie didn't hesitate. "He raped me."

Samantha held her tighter and shared her own history. "I'm a 'me too'. I was assaulted years ago."

Janie held Samantha tighter. "What happened?"

"I was assaulted during my medical residency."

"Did someone want to play doctor and you didn't?"

"Not exactly. I thought he was a good cop. Turned out, he was a bad cop."

"That sucks. Guess *to serve and protect* has a different meaning nowadays."

"I survived. It made headlines for days. No one wanted to believe a cop could be dirty."

"I met a good cop this week." Janie stated.

"Me too." Samantha sighed.

"He wanted to help me get out of here. I called him a prick. It felt like he could read my soul."

"I had a dinner date scheduled with mine, tonight."

"Then you're lucky because he'll be looking for you. All I had to offer the Indian cop was sex, and he refused."

"Did he have a name?" Samantha asked.

"Special Agent John Treehorn."

Samantha smiled. "He turned you down?"

"He didn't even consider it. He wore a ring. Lucky wife."

"He's widowed, and he's my dinner date."

"You lucky stiff."

"I swear if I get out of here, I'm going to sleep with him." Samantha promised.

"He asked?" Janie felt envious.

"No, but I think we were on the same path."

"He bought condoms." Janie let her know.

"I did, too." The women chuckled and went silent. Samantha wondered if she would ever use them.

"I'm scared." Janie whispered.

"Me too." Samantha agreed.

"This place smells like death." Janie said.

Samantha knew that too but refused to share it.

The girls heard the low rumble of a truck.

"I wonder if my sister waited at the bus station for me. I guess it doesn't matter, now."

Samantha felt faint. It would be hours before Treehorn searched for her.

"We're not going to make it out of here alive, are we?" Janie choked the words out.

Samantha offered her encouragement, "If your sister telephoned Agent Treehorn, it's only a matter of time before he finds us."

"Yes, but when he does, will we be dead or alive?" Janie asked as Brody opened the door.

Treehorn hung up his telephone. "There's no record Janie purchased a bus ticket."

Raven's fingers flew over the computer searching for the video files from the post office and surrounding area.

Treehorn examined the traffic camera that captured the view from the small courthouse.

Bobby Beltram arrived at the FBI office as the agents worked. "I apologize for intruding."

Treehorn shook Bobby's hand while Raven nodded. "No problem. What can we do for you?" The agent saw the man's reddened eyes and puffy face.

"Dr. Reynolds left a message with my voice mail. Do you know where she is? I called the morgue. She wasn't there."

"She may have been called out to a death."

"I'm sorry, Agent Treehorn, I didn't ask specifics. I came to see what information she had on Darcy's death and see if I could get an update from you, too."

Before Treehorn could respond Agent Wilson appeared at the doorway. "Dispatch just reported in. They sent Dr. Reynolds to a fatality that turned out to be a prank.

When they called to cancel she didn't respond. Her last known location was FBI housing."

Raven eyed Treehorn. "Go, I got this."

Treehorn sped to the FBI housing with full sirens and lights. He used his hands-free to telephone her. The call went to voicemail. "It's Treehorn, answer your phone." Cars and trucks cleared a path for him.

His vehicle slid to a stop in front of the lodging.

The agent's fist pounded on the doctor's door, "Samantha!" No response, only silence.

The cleaning staff hurried and unlocked the door to the obvious, vacant room.

He hit the redial on his phone and ran to examine her car. The agent heard a ringtone and watched as his face appeared on her phone from its location on the floorboard. Treehorn dialed 911 and identified him and his badge number: "Put an APB out on Dr. Samantha Reynolds, FBI Forensic Medical Examiner. Missing person. Send a CSU unit to FBI housing at 5th and Main. Dr. Reynolds's vehicle is here with her belongings locked inside."

Crime scene personnel worked the area as darkness fell. Treehorn didn't move from his position as he leaned against his vehicle, and neither did he interfere.

CSU Wilkerson approached with Samantha's possessions in evidence bags.

The agent signed the clipboard document and locked her items inside his vehicle.

"We'll let you know if we find anything."

Treehorn nodded and drove to his office. He telephoned Raven en route. "What did you find?"

"What's your ETA? I have the video and you need to see this."

"I just pulled in." Treehorn hurried into the building to locate his co-worker.

Raven was dressed in black tactical gear. "I pulled the post office surveillance and found Janie Nettles getting in a vehicle voluntarily at the post office." He stressed the point, "A *red* truck."

"Who owns it?" Treehorn demanded.

"Take a look." Raven pushed a letter on the keyboard and played the video.

Treehorn watched as a windshield view of the truck emerged. He watched a man strike Janie in the jaw. "Is that…?"

"…Brody Hauler," Raven confirmed. He clicked his keyboard and another camera angle highlighted the vehicle's license plate. He pointed to the printout. "DMV verified."

Treehorn examined the document. "Do you have the FBI lodging surveillance?"

"Yes," Raven typed. "Watch this." He activated the recording.

The agents watched as an unidentified red truck exited the FBI lot with no sign of Samantha.

"I don't believe in coincidences," Treehorn stated. "Put out an APB on Brody Hauler and his red truck," Treehorn ordered. "Assault with probable kidnapping."

"Already did for Janie and him before you arrived," Raven stated, "I have agents assigned to assist."

Treehorn stripped off his suit and dressed in the black tactical gear and equipment in the locker room.

The agent met the other men at the vehicles. "Let's find him and bury him."

Brody opened the dungeon door and turned on a second dim light bulb. He carried a brown paper bag. He removed a red dress and grey wig from the bag and handed them to Samantha. "Put them on."

"No."

He turned and slapped Janie on her bruised jaw.

Brody ordered Samantha, "Put the wig on."

"No."

He raised his arm to strike Janie again who moaned in pain.

"I'll put it on if you stop hitting her."

Brody handed the items to Samantha.

Samantha's chest muscles constricted when she saw Brody's dilated and drug-glazed eyes.

"Put them on."

Samantha grabbed the dress, turned around, and exchanged her shirt for the red dress.

Brody stroked one finger down her spine and very slowly zipped up the dress.

"Remove your pants."

Samantha's hands shook as she removed her dress pants but kept her underwear on.

"Now the wig," Brody ordered.

Her fingers trembled as she stuffed her hair under the putrid wig and gagged from its smell.

Brody's eyes followed his hands as they caressed the red dress, from her shoulders, down the chest, and over the hips. "Mommy," he muttered.

Samantha felt her chest start to constrict in a panic attack. "I'm not...."

"Shush." Brody placed his filthy hands over her lips, "No talking."

Janie was scared for Samantha and yelled, "She's not your mother!"

Brody turned, raised his fist, and punched Janie in the jaw. The bones that were weakened from his first punch fractured under the second strike. She crumpled in a heap.

Brody turned to Samantha and held out his hand for her to grasp.

Samantha's dilated eyes and open mouth showed her horror.

"Come on, I don't want to mess your hair."

Samantha stepped back from Brody.

"Do not walk away from me. You're always a disappointment. Do I need to get the belt out?"

"Please stop this." Samantha begged.

"You know how I hate to take the belt to you." Brody unbuckled his belt.

Samantha tried not to panic and whispered, "You don't need to use the belt."

Brody flexed his fists.

"You don't need to use your fists."

His smile didn't reach his crazy eyes. "I enjoy it when you're agreeable." He reached out his hand and Samantha's shook as she placed hers in his. Janie moaned, and Brody tightened his grip.

"Brody." Samantha whispered to get his attention.

He focused on the red dress. His calloused hands caressed the satin fabric.

"What would you like to talk about?" Samantha asked as she initiated a conversation.

He slapped her hard across the face in response. "You talk too much! How can a twelve-year-old talk so much?" and slapped her again on the same cheek.

"I won't say another word. I promise," Samantha whispered.

"Everyone makes promises. Harry said he'd stop hurting me. He never did. You made me promises; you didn't keep any of them. Come here."

Samantha resisted.

Brody grabbed her arm, pulled her, and slammed her face down on the table.

Samantha's panic attack caused her breath to come in short, shallow gasps.

Brody started rubbing her back. His rough hands slid effortlessly over the red satin dress. He tried to smooth out every wrinkle. He whispered in her ear, "You smell good."

She gasped for air.

His hands smoothed her back, over her hips and buttocks. "He's not going to find out."

Samantha's teeth chattered in fear, the same fear that prevented her from speaking.

Brody's hand's explored Samantha's legs and thighs beneath the dress.

"He's not going to find out." Brody whispered.

"Who's he?" She managed to ask.

"Harry. He's not going to find out, Mommy."

Brody's hands grabbed Samantha's underwear and tugged them down over her buttocks, down her legs. He forced her to move one leg, then the other, until he held her underwear in his palm. He folded them gently, smelled them, and placed them into his pocket.

Samantha prayed, *"Treehorn please save us,"* as she buried her face in the blanket that covered the table and smelled like death.

Chapter Fourteen

Louise Buckman's phone beeped. She rose off the pillow and reached for her phone on the nightstand and examined the message. "My medical examiner is missing." She pulled the strap of her lingerie up onto her shoulder as she stood up from the bed and picked up a cookie bag from the floor.

Robert Beltram relaxed against several pillows on his side of the king-sized bed. He took a long drag off his Cuban cigar from one hand while the other held a glass of his expensive Scotch.

Buckman's phone double-pinged and she examined the two messages. "Tell me about Brody Hauler," she asked as she dressed into her pants and blouse.

Beltram answered as he blew smoke rings, "Roughneck, he keeps the men in line."

Buckman reapplied her makeup in the bathroom mirror. "He's wanted for the assault of a missing prostitute." She washed her hands and the water pressure dropped. "There's an updated APB out on him and his red truck in a suspected kidnapping." She dried her hands and faced Beltram.

"You'd better find him before Agent Treehorn."

"Why's that?" Beltram asked as he took another puff of his Cuban cigar.

"Agent Treehorn will make a man sing like a bird. Any secrets someone has, the agent will get out of them, dead or alive."

"I have no control over my men if they break the law."

Buckman snapped at her rich lover. "I wasn't talking about your men."

Beltram puffed his cigar from his comfortable position and offered no reply.

Buckman's phone beeped again. "This night has become a nightmare. What else could happen?"

Beltram stood and pulled on his pants. "Louise...."

She interrupted him, "With all the money you have, could you at least hire a decent plumber to fix your water pressure?" Buckman grabbed her belongings and walked out.

"Louise...." He stood, alone. Beltram dressed and contemplated his options before deciding on a permanent course of action. The CEO looked out his bedroom window at his numerous natural gas wells, lit up like torches across the skyline as they flamed off excessive gases. He snuffed out his cigar and grabbed what he'd needed as he walked out of his expensive mansion to get his hands dirty.

Treehorn, Raven, and Agents Wilson and Garrand surrounded the dilapidated legal residence of Brody Hauler. Treehorn and Raven charged the front door with their weapons drawn, while the other two agents entered through the back. Their flashlights danced eerily in the darkened and vacant house as they searched all of its rooms.

"There's no one here." Treehorn's voice echoed in the empty house.

"Where is she?" Raven asked as the agents reholstered their weapons.

"Treehorn, please save me," Samantha whispered as she heard Brody's pants zipper being lowered. "What's Harry going to find out?" She asked loudly so it penetrated Brody's drug-hazed thoughts.

Brody heard her voice which added to the mantra in his head. "That I beat you and buried you alive under the old oak tree."

Samantha screamed and screamed, passed out, and fell to the floor.

Treehorn's shirt was soaked to the skin beneath his jacket. Samantha was going to die, and he couldn't save her, just like his deceased wife.

Raven eyed Treehorn and felt the sweat soak his own shirt. In all of his years, the one thing that remained true and constant, he'd never seen Treehorn panic, ever.

"It's the wrong place."

"Where's a map? Get us a map of the area, now!" Raven shouted.

One of the agents ran to his vehicle and returned with a map. They spread it out as their flashlights pinpointed their current location.

"Where is she?"

If Samantha had remained conscious, she would have heard Brody's phone ring and the sound of his pants being zipped up before he committed any deviant act.

"What's up, boss?" Brody asked as he walked out of his man cave and locked the door. He stuffed Samantha's underwear into the crematorium urn that sat front and center on his fireplace mantel. A metal container with an engraved name on the front: Harry Hauler. Brody zoned out of the telephone conversation as he remembered fondly the day his stepfather died.

"Brody!" Robert Beltram yelled, "Are you listening?"

"Yes!" Sarcasm laced his answer.

"Meet me at the cemetery. I have a body to bury," Beltram ordered.

"Right now?"

"Yes, it's urgent. Leave now and avoid the police."

"It's the last thing I'm doing for you tonight. I had plans," he snapped.

Brody gunned his engine as he drove away from his secondary residence. Red and blue lights lit up the far distance. The red lights triggered his childhood memories: at age ten the never-ending beatings from Harry with his wide, leather belt; age twelve the raping and sexual abuse at the hands of his mother; his years of begging, pleading, for her to stop; at age sixteen, burying his mother alive; the warning lights as he pushed the buttons at the crematorium that burned Harry alive, flashing like a broken recorder, forever playing the same tune in Brody's head, "He's going to find out!"

"I'm going to find him and bury him!" Treehorn reiterated. "I know someone who can help locate him." He telephoned Cookie Lighthouse. "This is Agent John Treehorn. May I please speak to Paco? I have a question for him."

"Sure, Mr. Treehorn. And, I just want to thank you. Whatever you said to my boy, he's been so good and has kept all of his promises to his momma." Paco smiled and looked sheepish as his mother turned to him, "Mr. Treehorn needs to ask you a question."

The little boy's voice came on the line, "Hello."

"Hi, Paco, do you remember the house you rode to in the red truck? We're here and there's no one home."

"It was dark in the back of the truck and bumpy."

"Think. Anything that may help."

"The barn door was scary."

"Barn door?" Treehorn and his agents were at a single house. Not a barn or shed in sight.

"Yes, it kept opening and closing in the wind. It scared me."

"Is there anything else?"

"Hmm…. Did you cross the bridge?"

"Bridge?"

"Yes, he drove over his bumpy lane and he crossed a bridge, because I heard the river."

"Thanks, Paco. I'm really proud of you and how you're keeping your promises to your mother."

"Thanks, Agent Treehorn."

Raven accessed satellite images of the area on his tablet while Treehorn spoke to the boy.

The agent terminated the call.

"Barn, lane, and a bridge over a river, Paco said." Treehorn repeated.

Raven zoomed in on their present location and zoomed out. Two inches away on the screen appeared two structures with a truck. Access to it was a long driveway over a bridge and river. "The two buildings are included on this residential property with a separate driveway." The agent scanned another reference page. "Same legal ownership."

"Follow me," Treehorn ordered the men as they ran to their SUVs.

He drove a mile down the road and turned into the driveway. It was bumpy. It took a couple of minutes, but soon the vehicles crossed a one-lane, wooden bridge over a small river. They approached the yard where a single light illuminated the two buildings. Treehorn's headlights illuminated one barn with its doors opened. No red truck was parked inside the barn or out, and it was deathly silent, too.

Brody drove into the cemetery, its wrought-iron fence kept in spirits and secrets. He drove past a marble mausoleum with "Beltram" engraved in its cold white marble. It appeared out of place both in the prairie setting and by the numerous simple wooden crosses that surrounded it.

Robert Beltram waited next to his Cadillac.

"You're going to have to enlarge this cemetery at the rate you're going."

"Maybe."

"Let's get this done. I have two ladies waiting for me."

Beltram raised a revolver and shot Brody in the stomach.

The man staggered back in shock, "Why?"

"The Feds found you. They're tearing your house apart right now. I can't have you talking or making a deal. That would be a disadvantage to me."

"I wouldn't, Father."

"I know." Robert Beltram raised his revolver and shot Brody dead-center in his forehead, blowing his brains out the back of his skull and killing the greatest psychopathic partner in crime, money did buy.

After he secured his gun in its vehicle compartment, he spoke to the corpse, "You were never my son; you were my bastard." Beltram's only regret was that Brody should have dug his own grave before taking a bullet. The CEO didn't do physical labor.

Brody's cold dead eyes watched as the man who provided his life seed and end bullet dug a shallow grave, removed his belongings from his pockets, and covered him with dirt. Beltram didn't care if the wolves dragged the body away in a couple days. No one was going to care about a dead serial killer.

Beltram dialed another potential mentee. "Jameson, congratulations, you've been promoted." He listened to the response and interrupted, "I have a job for you. Brody Hauler's truck is near the entrance to the Beltram cemetery. The feds are searching for him and his truck. I sent him to another operation until things blow over, but I promised him we'd get rid of the truck. He left me the keys. I want you to drive it to the welding building, cut it into pieces and bury them. Do you understand?" He waited for the response. "Pick it up now with someone you trust. Get it done and buried by sunrise, and we'll discuss your promotion."

"Yes, boss," replied Jameson, the eager employee.

Beltram drove Brody's truck to the road and left the keys in it. He meticulously used his handkerchief to wipe his fingerprints off the truck. He hauled his Scotch-laden rear up the hill and climbed into his Cadillac and thought, '*What a nightmare!*'

Treehorn and the other agents stepped from their vehicles with their guns drawn.

Once again Treehorn and Raven entered through the front door, while Wilson and Garrand charged the rear of the structure.

The building was clearly lived in and filthy. It contained one TV with a Barcalounger, a small kitchen, and a bathroom. Above was a sleeping loft that contained one bed and an overstuffed closet.

Treehorn ordered the two agents, "Go check the outside barn."

The agents combed the house for clues. A paystub bearing Brody Hauler's name lay on the kitchen counter. They searched structure room by room. It didn't take long.

Treehorn shouted, "Samantha!" Silence. "Janie!"
Silence.

"Could he have them in the barn?" Raven asked.

Wilson and Garrand returned from their outside duty,
"No one's in there."

Treehorn holstered his weapon, sat down, and bowed
his head. He couldn't save his wife and now he was going
to lose another woman he cared for. He stood and offered
a prayer to the Creator to guide him. When he opened his
eyes, he realized he was staring at a loft that was larger than
the rooms beneath it. He pointed to the rear of the
structure. "A hidden room."

Treehorn pulled his weapon again and turned on his
flashlight. Raven followed on his heels. Wilson and
Garrand ran outside and examined the perimeter wall of the
structure.

A partition slid sideways, hidden behind a solid iron
door. A nail embedded in the door frame held a single key.
Treehorn removed it, and his hand shook as he inserted it
into the lock. The only outward sign that he cared.

The door swung open.

Treehorn flicked the switch and one light bulb did
little to illuminate the room.

Two women lay motionless on the floor. Treehorn recognized Janie Marie Nettles. The other was a grey-haired woman in a red dress. No Samantha.

Raven grabbed a blanket and covered Janie. He felt for a pulse, "She's alive." He dialed 911, "FBI Agent Raven Shelly, we need an ambulance at 305 Brook Lane."

Treehorn approached the other woman who was lying face down. Who was she? He felt for a pulse. "This one's alive, too. Tell them we have two to transport."

Raven nodded. "We need two ambulances to transport two female trauma victims."

Treehorn shined the flashlight on her face and recognized, "Samantha!"

She refused to open her eyes in her nightmare.

"Sam," whispered Treehorn.

"Cover her with your jacket. She's probably in shock," Raven ordered.

Treehorn removed his jacket and covered her. His flashlight illuminated her bruised and swollen cheek. Someone had slapped her, hard. "Sam, the ambulances are on their way."

Samantha inhaled his scent from the jacket, it wasn't a dream.

"Treehorn?"

"Yes."

"How did you find us?"

"Cookie crumbs. Are you hurt? Can you move, Doc?"

"He slapped me."

"I can see that."

"Treehorn?"

"Yes." The man gently comforted her.

"He took my underwear."

Treehorn smiled, she was all right. "I can't see that."

"I want you to," she whispered. Then, louder she asked, "Can you help me up?"

Treehorn assisted her and helped her put her arms into the jacket sleeves. He zipped it up, so it would stay on her. "You okay?"

She yanked the wig off. Her face showed disgust for it.

Treehorn wrapped his arms around her. "I've got you."

Samantha pulled back, grabbed his face, and gave him a kiss. She wrapped her arms tight around him to make sure that he was real and inhaled his unique, musky natural scent. "Thank you."

"You're welcome."

Samantha saw Raven treating Janie. "Don't move her. Brody knocked her out with a fist to the jaw. It's probably broken." The doctor left the comfort of Treehorn's arms to tend to Janie.

Raven and Treehorn stepped back and watched.

"Can you tell the ambulance we'll need a neck-brace cervical collar immediately when they arrive? Cancel the second ambulance, I don't need one."

"Are you sure?"

"It was just a slap. I'll put some ice on it and it'll be fine."

"Were you unconscious?"

"I fainted from a panic attack."

Ambulance sirens approached. Treehorn motioned Raven outside. "Cancel the other ambulance and get what she needs."

Treehorn watched as Samantha treated Janie's injuries.

"We survived," Samantha whispered softly to Janie.

Agent Wilson and Garrand listened to Treehorn's orders. "I'm taking the doctor to the hospital. Shelly's in charge. I want that man caught, understood?" Treehorn watched as Raven returned, neck brace and ice in hand.

Samantha gently placed the brace around Janie's neck as she moaned. "You're going to be fine. One day this will be history. Don't let it affect your life." Janie blinked in understanding.

She tried to speak but her broken jaw prevented her.

Treehorn squeezed Janie's hand, "You have your sister to thank. She called me when you didn't arrive on the shuttle."

Janie tightened her hold on his hand.

He leaned in closer and whispered, "Thank you for Donovan."

Her eyes widened, and she winked.

The ambulance staff secured Janie to the backboard, then onto the stretcher. The male and female EMTs were professional and kind. The agents watched as the gurney was wheeled toward the ambulance. Once it was secured, the ambulance doors slammed, and the vehicle departed.

Treehorn handed Samantha an ice pack which she gratefully put on her swollen and bruised cheek. "Let me take you to the hospital."

"I'm fine. I want to get out of these clothes." She placed her hand on his arm, "Can you please drive me to the lodging?"

"Raven, you're in charge. You have CSU examine every inch of this place. I don't care how long it takes or the number of staff members it needs. Contact Mancuso if you need anything or have a problem. Let Buckman know what went down, but I think she already knows."

Raven nodded once at the orders. It was the first time his fellow agent and friend had departed a crime scene early and left another in charge.

Chapter Fifteen

Treehorn removed the evidence bag that contained Samantha's purse, keys, and telephone from the secured compartment in his vehicle and handed them to her.

She checked her belongings. Nothing was missing: wallet, keys, gun, stun gun, and her pepper spray. She examined the items and thought, '*A lot of good they did inside my purse*'. "Let's go."

Treehorn helped her into his vehicle, then sat in the driver's seat, but didn't start the engine. "I'm here if you want to talk or not talk," The man gently offered.

"I prayed for you to save me," Samantha whispered.

The agent drove them to the lodging, the police radio kept them updated with the current events.

Samantha handed Treehorn the key to her room. He unlocked her door and helped her inside. The man examined her bruised face. "Are you sure you don't want that x-rayed, Doc?"

"I'm sure. I want a hot shower, a beer, and bed in that order. I'll write my statement in the morning."

Treehorn nodded. He went in the bathroom and turned on the hot shower. The lodging may be ancient, but the hot water system was new and provided an endless supply. To hell with the water bill tonight.

Samantha gathered her pajamas and an evidence bag.

"Do you need anything?" Treehorn gently asked.

"I don't have any beer."

Samantha's shadowed eyes told the story. The shock had set in.

"I'll get the beer while you shower. Take your time. I have your key."

Samantha closed the bathroom door. She carefully removed the satin dress and placed it into the plastic evidence bag. The hot water blended with the tears as they streamed down her face. No amount of water would wash away the fright she experienced tonight but she let it try.

Treehorn heard her enter the shower, then he moved. He grabbed his jacket, locked the door, and hurried to his room. He stripped and showered in less than five minutes, then hurriedly dressed in jeans, shirts, and sneakers. He grabbed his weapon, ID, handcuffs, and his phone. He removed a cold six-pack from the refrigerator. He looked around his lodging. Everything was secured.

He hurried out of his room. The shower was still running when he arrived so he removed two beers and placed the remainder in the refrigerator.

Treehorn knocked on the bathroom door. "How are you doing?"

"I'll be right out."

Treehorn felt himself harden as he visualized Samantha naked in the shower. He sat in the chair and placed his cold beer between his legs. He was a sick son of a bitch. He wasn't going to touch her, even if it killed him.

He picked up his phone and texted his lover in Washington, he owed her. *I met someone.*

Odette Wilson, a John Hopkins trained psychotherapist, had helped him pick up the pieces of his life after the death of his wife. She knew Treehorn, or more precisely the man he wanted her to know. She approved his FBI entrance psychological examination, relinquished her professional ties to him, and became his lover. It was remarkable that the relationship had lasted over a decade. He was her dinner date when she needed one, and she was his. His sexual needs were met, and he made sure hers were, too. Treehorn knew she had other lovers. That was her prerogative. It wasn't a love match; it was a convenience.

He had his job, and he didn't realize he needed more until he met Samantha, when something shifted inside him.

His phone beeped a few seconds later from Odette, *"And?"*

"I want more." He sent the message. He had no regrets. He knew Odette would be there for him if he ever needed her.

On the other end, Treehorn's forty-five-year-old friend, lover, and ex-therapist read her text and smiled.

"Good news?" asked her very late-night dinner date.

"Yes. A friend of mine finally found what he's been searching for, a little speck of happiness in this cruel world." Odette smiled at the very rich and powerful man who sat across from her as they sipped their post-dinner drinks. She was surprised that she had enjoyed her time with him. He made no secret that he desired her. She doubted if any man could perform better than Treehorn in the sack, but money was a factor at her age. "Let's go back to my place." She sent Treehorn a final text.

The agent's phone pinged, *"Shed the shirt! GOOD LUCK!"* He smiled and shut his phone off as the door *clicked* and Samantha entered the room.

Her red hair curled gently around her freckled face. Dressed in a white T-shirt and plaid pajamas she looked ten years younger. She dumped the red dress inside its evidence bag onto her dresser.

Treehorn opened a beer and handed it to her.

"Thanks." She took a long and satisfying swallow.

The man watched her throat muscles contract as the beer went down. He placed his beer on his zipper. The mantra echoed in his head, *I'm not going to touch her even if it kills me.*

They both felt the sexual tension in the room and neither made a move to alleviate it. Two damaged victims unwilling to test the waters as they wore their white matching T-shirts.

The agent finished his beer. "Do you have your phone handy?" He stood to leave. "You can call me if you need anything during the night."

"Can you stay a little longer?" Samantha's voice sounded like a plea.

Treehorn felt like a masochist at this point. "Sure."

"Do you want another beer?"

"No, I'm set."

Samantha left one bedside lamp on and crawled under the blankets. The white sheet was a sharp contrast to her red hair and freckled complexion. "Can you lie next to me until I fall asleep?"

"Are you sure?" *I'm not going to touch her even if it kills me.* Treehorn stretched out on top of the blankets.

Samantha rolled over so that she was against Treehorn.

He put his arm around her. "Go to sleep."

Treehorn closed his eyes and felt her relax as her breathing deepened to sleep. He needed to rise but his body refused. She snuggled deeper against him and sleep claimed him. He hadn't slept in the arms of any woman since his wife, not even with Odette. They had sex, then they returned to their respective apartments. He closed his eyes and surrendered to his feelings, to his dreams.

The sunshine and waterfall were as beautiful as he remembered them. He watched as Skyler walked toward him, not in her wedding dress but in the red dress he buried her. Samuel and Treehorn's parents, Anna Treehorn and John Wellington, all watched Skyler with love and pride shining in their eyes. Treehorn looked to his parents for guidance. They smiled and nodded. Skyler walked up to Treehorn and placed her hands on his smooth cheeks as love shined from her beautiful brown eyes, looked deep into his, and whispered, "I'm happy for you."

Treehorn's eyes flew open. The bedside clock showed, 3:10. He got up and used the bathroom and returned to the room. He contemplated returning to his room when Samantha spoke, "Come back to bed."

I'm not going to touch her even if it kills me. Treehorn left the light on and stretched out his long form next to Samantha.

She moved her hand beneath Treehorn's T-shirt and his abs involuntarily tightened.

"Recovery sex is bad." The man removed her hand and placed it on top of his T-shirt and hugged her.

"Is that what it's called?" Samantha let out a deep sigh, a victim's sigh. She was ready to tell him because she knew he would never ask.

"I don't need to know."

"I was in my doctoral residency at the University of Virginia. I was at a crime scene and I met a cop who had a thing for redheads. We went out a couple of times; he was the epitome of 'to serve and protect'. We went to a cop bar and to his place. I believe he drugged me, but I couldn't prove it. I woke up and he was on top of me, assaulting me. My chest was covered in bruises; he got off on that. I went straight to the hospital. His female partner conveniently misplaced my rape kit, the drug samples, everything I needed to convict him. My family was very supportive. Medication and a rape counselor have helped, but I've experienced panic attacks whenever I've felt trapped. It's been four years. He took a piece of me that night that I've never gotten back. I don't know if I ever will and that's what angers me. I carry a gun, pepper spray, and defensive items in my purse when I leave my lodging. Brody Hauler showed me they offered me little protection when needed."

"Give me his name and I'll kill him." Treehorn stated.

Samantha hoped he joked, "I would prefer it if he and his sidekick could feel the pain their victims have felt, then go to prison for their crimes."

"I'm sorry."

"I just want to feel normal."

Samantha put her hand under Treehorn's T-shirt again and popped the button on his jeans.

His hand covered and stopped it from moving. "Have you been with anyone since?"

Samantha eyes couldn't meet his. "No."

Treehorn leaned over and kissed her, and she stiffened. "I can't…"

Treehorn rolled back onto his back, "I know, Samantha."

She finished the sentence she started, "I panic…"

Treehorn stood up. "It's okay."

"Please, don't leave." Samantha begged and hated herself for doing it.

"I'm not. I have something that will help." Treehorn turned around and held up his handcuffs.

Samantha's chest contracted painfully and she broke out in a sweat. "How will those help?"

Treehorn became serious. "They're not for you, they're for me." He placed one handcuff on his wrist, stretched out again on the bed, swung the other cuff around the metal headboard, and secured the cuff to his other wrist.

"You decide how this is going to precede, Samantha. Just don't misplace the key because I don't want to write *that* incident report."

A tear rolled down her face as she rolled out of bed. "I'll be right back."

She brushed her teeth. Her anti-anxiety pills sat on the edge of her sink next to her vitamins. Could she do this? Samantha picked up the bottle, opened a drawer and placed it inside without opening the container.

She approached Treehorn, six feet of masculinity, and her chest contracted. Samantha softly grasped his cheeks and lowered her mouth for a kiss. A fresh-minty kiss and it tasted like paradise.

She lifted her leg and straddled his groin.

He groaned as he fists clenched the metal headboard railing.

"I want your T-shirt off."

"No." He didn't want his scars affecting this night.

"Too bad, I'm in control and those handcuffs pretty much limit your decision-making ability." Samantha lowered her hands and Treehorn lifted his body so she could move the T-shirt. She took her time, caressing every rib as she pushed the shirt over his muscular abs, up toward his nipples, over his head, and up his arms. The handcuffs prevented full removal. He took advantage of her location and kissed her breast through her T-shirt.

"You like that?" She lowered her mouth to his nipples, sucked and licked. The black and blue bruise on his ribs was swollen. Samantha kissed that too.

Treehorn felt his temperature rise, "We have a medical problem."

"I'm a doctor. Maybe I can help."

"I don't have any condoms here."

"I have condoms, and I'm on the pill." She wiggled her ass causing Treehorn to harden substantially.

"Why do you have condoms?" he asked.

"I purchased them the day after you arrived and I'm on the pill to regulate my periods." Samantha continued with her empowering movement and friction on top as she examined Treehorn's beautiful face, his black hair, and brown-blue eyes. She wanted and needed to see his face at all times, so she left the lamp on.

"Samantha." He groaned her name.

She wiggled some more. "Yes?"

A fine sheen covered Treehorn.

She rubbed his jeans.

He wasn't going to survive the night much less a minute more of her wiggling. "I need a condom on right now."

She removed his pants and complied with his request.

The first time they made love Treehorn's hands remained cuffed. She was scared. He soothed her fears with his calm voice. He came too quickly, she didn't come at all.

Treehorn held her while she cried herself to sleep and vowed he would track down the man who had violated her. As he held her he thought of them, two victims, him in his T-shirt and boxers; her in a T-shirt and plaid pajamas. Would it ever be right?

He kissed her awake.

The second time they made love the handcuffs were replaced with his caressing hands. They surrendered their trusted T-shirts. His strong hands brought life into her broken spirit while hers sought to soothe his. They believed they had touched a little sliver of heaven, and later, slept peacefully wrapped in each other's arms.

Chapter Sixteen

Treehorn's phone beeped at 6 am. He pulled on his jeans and examined a message that read, *"All male agents are to report to the office, NOW. FBI Supervisor Louise Buckman."*

A second message arrived immediately from Raven, *"Coffee?"*

Treehorn texted, *'Yes.'*

Raven texted, *"I'm outside."*

Treehorn texted, *"Don't say a word."*

Raven examined the cryptic message twice.

Treehorn gathered his weapon, ID, and belongings. He leaned over and kissed Samantha on her brow instead of her bruised cheek, "Work calls."

She hugged his pillow and watched with one eye as his long legs carried him out of her room. Samantha inhaled his musky scent from the pillow and snuggled into the blankets.

Raven watched as Treehorn walked out of Samantha's room instead of his own. His shirt tails flapped in the wind.

"Don't say a word and don't ever mention her body parts again." Treehorn threatened his friend.

Raven smiled. He understood the message and knew it would never be discussed, well maybe.

Treehorn unlocked his door, dressed quickly, secured his equipment, and headed out the door before the coffee that waited for him cooled.

"Did you get Buckman's message?" Raven asked as he handed Treehorn his drink.

"Any clue as to what happened?"

"No, but we'll find out soon enough."

The FBI office parking lot was filled with every company vehicle. Both agents knew this indicated something serious had happened that required all of the staff to report to duty in-house.

The office had become an active crime scene. Investigators and Internal Affair's suits swarmed the offices.

Treehorn and Raven passed the older coroner, Dr. William Ryder, as he and his staff wheeled two gurneys with matching black body bags out the door.

Buckman motioned to the two agents as soon as she saw their arrival. "Donovan and detention guard Weldon

Rivers were shot and killed here last night by a male assailant."

Treehorn remained silent while Raven whistled.

"Everyone's being tested." Buckman pointed the men toward the lab. She believed anyone could be a suspect until cleared by their lab.

The agent kept his investigative opinion to himself.

Treehorn and Raven entered the lab and completed the required forms with their name and badge numbers. They were required to list where they were between the hours of 10 pm to 3 am.

Dorris conducted the gunshot residue test on Raven while Anita tested Treehorn.

They hadn't fired their weapons, so they knew the test would be negative and their alibis were solid since they were at Brody's house and FBI housing during the time frame.

Dorris informed Raven, "You're free to go."

Anita informed Treehorn, "You're cleared too."

"What happened to Donovan and Weldon?" Treehorn asked after the lab had emptied out of other personnel.

Anita answered, "Donovan, small caliber with silencer, five shots, and triangulated." Anita used herself as a target in the way only a seasoned lab tech could describe the multiple bullet's entry points. "What we found unique, was the throat shot was done first to silence Donovan, then the right lung, next the heart, and last, the two to the eyes. It was definitely an execution."

Dorris added, "I'll lay money someone has that MO on a coroner's report somewhere. Weldon took one to the head, deadly and efficient."

Anita handed Treehorn a document. "Here are the results from the water samples tested."

Treehorn read the results and passed it to Raven.

The lab tech handed Treehorn a hand-sized box labeled "Property of the FBI."

The agent opened it. It contained two plastic bags labeled "EVIDENCE" with serial tracking numbers. He handed it to Raven.

Anita handed Treehorn a document to sign transferring the evidence to him.

He scribbled his signature.

The tech handed Treehorn an additional report, "They've been fingerprinted. Only one had a print obviously and it's a match from the documentation Agent Shelly provided."

"Thank you."

The women nodded at their accomplishments. They knew someone would soon be arrested for murder.

Raven asked his co-worker outside the lab, "Are you going to assist Buckman with Donovan?"

Treehorn wasn't in a helping mood. "It's her mess to clean up."

The two agents went to their office and closed their door. They had enough to focus on without Buckman's investigation interrupting them.

Raven made coffee. He didn't tell Treehorn he had refused to leave Brody's house as he supervised the CSU and his fellow agents. He'd survive on no sleep, again.

The agent handed Treehorn the primary information gathered. "CSU removed forty-two pairs of underwear from a crematorium container that we assume held the ashes of one Harry Hauler. I assume five of the underwear belonged to Darcy, Sandy, Janie, Dr. Reynolds, and one other that had her name tagged from Valley County Jail, Nichelle Walters."

"I want an FBI agent accompanying the underwear to the University of Arizona labs for testing today. I'll put the call in myself to the director. I want those results ASAP," Treehorn ordered.

"They're already on a plane to Tucson with the wig." Raven might be a pisser at times but he was first rate investigator who didn't need to be micromanaged. He made good coffee too, and handed his friend a refill.

"What did you find on Brody Hauler?" Treehorn examined the women on the bulletin board. "Samantha told me Brody confessed to killing both his mother and stepfather. Someone that crazy should have a psychiatric record or history."

"Yes, he did. A judge agreed and opened his sealed juvenile record." Raven handed it to Treehorn. "It's filled with documentation of years of abuse that started when the kid was young. He had periods of removal to foster care and treatment facilities. At age twelve it appeared he suffered his first psychotic break. A social worker suspected possible sexual abuse by his mother. The kid never confessed anything. The file contains pages of documentation from staff on their observations. Not one word from the kid. Not one conversation ever recorded with another patient. Nothing."

"What else?" Treehorn knew Raven would have netted the data needed to answer any question.

"Here's his birth certificate."

Treehorn read it and confirmed what both agents suspected.

"Here's an interesting detail." Raven handed Treehorn a photo. "When foster care removed Brody from his house, on several occasions he would always be found in this one location. One of the social workers took these pictures."

The agent examined them. The first black and white image showed a leafless tree that appeared to be used as a laundry line. A single dress appeared attached to its branch, not to the string. The next image, the photographer had stepped back ten feet, and the next ten feet more. That image included a stream. The agent recognized the duplicated scene. "It's Darcy Clearwater's body dump location re-enacted."

Raven added, "Yes, now look at the last image."

Treehorn flipped to the final photo. A pair of rusty metal wrist cuffs was embedded into the bark of the tree. "The kid was beaten and only the Creator knows what else."

"Any hits on the APB?" Treehorn examined the map.

"Roadblocks were set up twenty miles outside of town on every highway. State Troopers were ordered to check every ID. Neither he nor his truck has left the area.

"We'll find him, and then, I'll bury him." Treehorn wouldn't stop until he achieved that goal.

"Buckman won't be pleased to know that we've identified a serial killer in her jurisdiction."

"I think she suspected it and connected it to Lakken Energy a long time ago but refused to investigate." Treehorn added, "Too many women have gone missing in the area, and every single one of their families deserves an explanation."

"I've assumed Brody killed Sandy," Raven stated.

Treehorn nodded once, "Yes, but he didn't kill Darcy, Paco confirmed that. Brody transported her body from the apartment to his residence. Paco said, 'he heard screaming from Brody's house.' I think that was Sandy screaming. He killed her and dumped her at the same site and left my name on her as a message."

Raven said, "We know he's going to prison for the kidnapping of Janie Nettles and Dr. Reynolds."

"That's a fact, and it's the start to end of our job here," Treehorn added as he examined the bulletin board.

Raven smiled. His fellow agent would have his handcuffs in hand today for a murderer.

The agent examined Darcy's and Sandy's photos on the bulletin board.

"What are you thinking?"

"What I've suspected. Two killers. Two serial killers. Brody Hauler was one, his father is the other."

"How do we prove it beyond what we already have?"

"Evidence."

"What are you thinking?" Raven had seen that look in his friend's eyes before.

"List the Lakken employees and their criminal files that I know you've researched."

Raven sat at his computer and his fingers flew across the keyboard. A large plasma screen lit up on the wall. "Where do you want me to start with the crime-loving deviants?"

"Open cases," Treehorn replied.

"Fourteen investigations for murder or manslaughter, one hundred twenty-six for assault, and two hundred twenty drug-related cases. Do you want me to break down the prostitution, petty larcenies, and disorderly conduct?"

"No." Treehorn examined the numbers on the board. "Keep the prostitution file but remove the others."

271

Raven deleted the information from the screen.

"Now, Lakken Operation locations."

Raven typed, and the information appeared on the screen.

"Add the MMIW women who disappeared at, or near, their locations."

Raven worked the keyboard.

"Remove active investigations where there's a suspect," Treehorn requested.

More clicks.

"Remove suspected runaways."

More faces disappeared from the screen.

"Remove anyone with a history of attempted suicide."

A few more faces disappeared.

"List the remaining women by ages."

Women appeared on the screen.

"Remove the four elderly women on the far right," Treehorn added.

Twenty-four women's faces stared at the two agents. Treehorn's profile emerged.

"Oh, my God," uttered Raven as he examined the women.

"Add their dates of disappearance."

Raven's fingers typed the information.

"Now put them in chronological order of date reported missing," Treehorn added.

"Stolen Sisters," Raven said.

Twenty-four women the agents hadn't known before today, but four they did.

"You found it."

Treehorn identified a serial killer, his possible victims, and his motive. They were all red-headed including Janie Nettles, but not the other three: Nichelle Walters, Sandy Begay, or Darcy Clearwater.

Raven added one more photo to the list. Brenda Beltram and her date of death. "Robert Beltram's wife's death was the trigger that started this and Hanna Redmond appears to be the last red-haired woman reported missing."

"Did you provide any information to Bobby Beltram when I went in search of Samantha?"

"No, he said he'd wait to hear from the doctor."

"I'll arrange a meeting with him at Darcy's apartment."

Bobby Beltram opened the apartment door when Treehorn arrived. "Come in. I was just packing a few personal items."

The Navajo agent noticed the wedding basket sat safely on top of the box.

"I made a fresh pot of coffee. Want a cup?"

Treehorn nodded, "Black."

Bobby started to talk. "I met Darcy at 8:15 am on the day she interviewed for the job. Did you ever meet someone and it was an instant attraction?"

"Yes," Treehorn thought of Samantha, "I've known the feeling."

"It was like that. We fought the attraction. We argued about it and we surrendered to it. She refused my marriage offer. She said, it was just an attraction and it would burn out." Bobby sipped his coffee. "It burned brighter. How was that possible?"

Treehorn watched as Bobby disappeared into his memories.

"She didn't want to love a white man and I knew my father would never accept an Indian. My mother was killed by one, Agent Treehorn. He never recovered from his loss. There was an oil well incident on the ridge one day. Darcy investigated it. When she came home she finally agreed to marry me. She said our time here is short. We flew to the Navajo Reservation the next day and had a private ceremony. We didn't tell a soul. My father didn't know that I had married. No one knew."

"I believe her killer knew. Tell me about Lakken history."

"My grandfather was a wildcatter out of Texas. He paid for my father's geology degree. He always stated that you need two things to find oil in the ground, education and luck. My father always suspected there was oil in this region after years working the Canadian energy fields. He was one of the first to set up test wells. They paid off. He had money, he used it to acquire the oil and mineral rights, and as they say, the rest is history."

"When were you going to inform your father about your marriage?"

"Darcy and I were discussing an appropriate time."

"What do you think would happen if your father found out that you married an Indian?"

"He'd probably be angry or disappointed."

"Would he disown you? Fire you?"

"He's threatened to disown me every time we've had an argument about an environmental issue, Agent Treehorn. He's welcome to fire me. My mother left me a trust fund upon her death. Her father was the wildcatter. I have a lifetime of money. I don't need a cent from my father."

"Would he be angry enough to kill?"

"My father couldn't kill anyone. He's always loved and protected me, Agent Treehorn."

Treehorn thought about Robert Beltram. He would get his hands dirty and he'd pay for someone to kill, someone like his second son. "What can you tell me about Brody Hauler?"

"Father's right-hand man. He works the men hard but that's his job - to keep them in line and make my father more money." Treehorn noticed that he didn't use the past tense.

"How long has he worked for your father?" The agent asked.

"He arrived here when he was a teenager. I don't know why my father took him on. Brody was the first person he hired who wasn't legal age."

"Do you know why Darcy asked for me?" Treehorn wanted to know if Bobby covered for his father's activities.

"She never mentioned you, other than to comment on the *Indian Times* on her bulletin board. Darcy said, "There's an agent who would never give up. She admired you for that."

"The *Indian Times* identified me as an FBI agent. She left me a note. Was there anything illegal going on that she wanted me to investigate?"

"She never told me. Did she put herself in danger?"

Treehorn remained silent.

"Let's retrace Darcy's movements the day she died," Treehorn started. "She left work and traveled to Granite Ridge. You met at her apartment and you had sex. She left her computer there and carried her phone. You rode with her to the MMIW dinner but left for your emergency."

"Yes," Bobby agreed on the timeline.

"She received a threatening telephone call at the party which visibly upset her."

"Who called her?"

"Her killer. She returned home and called you at 8:15 and left a message on your voicemail. We were led to believe she was killed for her activism with the Missing and Murdered Indigenous Women's Movement. I know that wasn't the case."

"Who killed her?" Bobby whispered.

Treehorn continued without answering him, "She returned here to the apartment with her award, but what the killer didn't know was that she wasn't alone."

"Who killed my wife?" Bobby's anger increased.

The agent continued, "She emailed a file from her computer to her phone which she password protected."

"What file?" Bobby asked.

Treehorn still didn't answer any of Bobby's questions. "Darcy sat here and saw the arrival of her killer. She wrote my name on a note, stuck it to her phone, and gave it to her guest. My picture was on the cover of the *Indian Times*. She knew I wouldn't give up on a crime regardless of how long it took to find justice."

"What happened?" Bobby asked as his face reddened with anger.

"Her phone contains the motive of her death. The man struck her which caused her to fall and hit her neck."

"You know who killed her."

"And so do you," Treehorn continued. "The killer stomped on her wrist, not only killing time, but specifically so he could remove the one possession that meant the world to him, his wife's wedding ring. The same ring you gave Darcy when you married."

Bobby's face paled as shock and realization struck him as to the killer's identity.

"Agent Shelly executed a search warrant yesterday and recovered the two items only the killer would have in his possession."

Raven banged the knocker on an expensive front door, while he held his badge and warrant in the other.

Kaya Massey opened Robert Beltram's front door. Raven served her the search warrant. She opened the door wider and allowed Raven, Agent Wilson, and CSU Wilkerson entry into the home.

Raven witnessed as CSU Wilkerson searched a closet.

She examined each brown leather shoe until she found what she was searching for and placed the pair into an evidence bag. She made a quick search of his bedroom desk and nightstands. "It's not here."

"Check the study." Raven accompanied her to Beltram's office where she searched his desk. "I found it." Wilkerson removed an item from the drawer and placed it in bag labeled "EVIDENCE".

Kaya Massey held open the front door as the FBI staff exited the house, "He'll get what's coming to him one day."

"They always do," Raven replied as he zipped up his jacket in the falling snow.

"How did she end up next to a ditch?" Bobby asked.

"Your father called his right-hand man who moved the body, who washed her, sodomized her, and accidentally redressed her in another woman's dress."

"Who?" Bobby guessed, but wanted it said.

"Your half-brother, Brody Hauler."

Bobby turned a shade paler and pushed his coffee away.

Treehorn waited for the man to compose himself. "Darcy went to Granite Ridge, repeatedly. I wanted to see why."

"What did the earthquakes show?"

"She found the illegal activity."

"What?"

"Activity that went against her beliefs and against her environmental engineering. It was why she was killed."

"Tell me."

Treehorn pulled out Darcy's phone and activated it. He typed in 0815 and looked at the spaces of her password. On Darcy's desk sat her 'TRIDENT' award. The agent typed it into her phone and it unlocked it. He clicked her email icon and opened the document. "She wrote a detailed report about Lakken's groundwater contamination at Granite Ridge."

"Please tell me he didn't kill my wife."

Treehorn drilled home the crime, "He killed your wife who carried your unborn child. Your half-brother dumped her body in a snowbank; all because she found out your father was illegally dumping chemicals into the aquifer thus contaminating the groundwater."

"I'm going to kill him. I'll kill both of them."

"You know I can't allow that."

"Who's going to stop me?"

The agent walked to the door and opened it. Troopers Allen and Maresca stood outside. "These troopers will stay here until your father's taken into custody."

Treehorn removed Bobby's cell phone from his pocket and handed it to Trooper Allen. "I can't allow you to contact your father and warn him. My fellow agents and I will arrest him. He'll pay for the crimes he committed."

"Why, Agent Treehorn? Why would he harm the Indians? This community? Their water supply?"

"What is the one thing your father values more than anything?"

"Money? He did this for the money!"

"Yes, and I suspect there was one other reason. I'll ask him when I arrest him." Treehorn transferred Darcy's file to his phone for safe keeping and turned it off. He touched her TRIDENT award for the last time before exiting the apartment.

Howie knocked on Robert Beltram's office door to update the CEO of Darcy's telephone activation and new location.

Ruth answered the office door. "He's not here."

Chapter Seventeen

Treehorn, Raven, and four other agents walked out of their office building dressed in black fatigues with FBI labeled on their bulletproof vests. They checked their weapons, gear, and loaded into three vehicles. No one at the office questioned the imminent arrest. The place still swarmed with officials and agents investigating the two murders.

Raven watched the scenery pass as Treehorn drove. He felt the calm before the storm, as every agent knew an arrest could go sideways at any given moment. He offered a prayer to the Creator as he pictured Dana's face and his two children. Raven glanced at Treehorn and wondered where his thoughts were as they crossed the prairie to make the arrest.

In the past, Treehorn thought of his parents and Skyler. Today, it was Samantha's arms wrapped around his soul, and he knew it could get him killed.

The three FBI vehicles parked next to the garage. Agents Anderson and Wilson ran to the rear of the house while another waylaid an older man carrying trash to the outside bin. Treehorn, Raven, and Agent Morales filed to the front door. Agent Garrand surveyed the perimeter.

A uniformed Hispanic woman opened the door and her shock silenced her. Treehorn waved her out and whispered, "¿Habla usted Inglés?"

"Yes. Mr. Beltram requires me to speak English."

"We're FBI. What's your name?"

"Maria Espinosa."

"Maria, how many people are here?" The agent watched her face for honesty.

"Just Luis, my husband", the maid pointed to the man with the trash, "and Mr. Beltram, that I know of."

Treehorn observed an older vehicle in the driveway. "Is that your car?"

Maria nodded.

"I want you to go with this agent. He'll take you and Luis to a safe location. Where's Mr. Beltram?"

"He's in the study." The maid pointed to a hallway located off the main foyer.

Treehorn motioned for Agent Morales to escort the woman to her husband. "Keep them warm and safe." He then waved Garrand over to join them.

Raven whispered into his throat microphone to the two agents at the rear of the house, "Anderson and Wilson, the suspect is in his study near the front entrance. Treehorn and I will take the study; Garrand will enter from the front of the house and unlock the rear door. You three are in charge with securing the remaining rooms. Morales has two of the known occupants safe and secured outside of the house."

The agents crossed the foyer with their weapons raised. They crept down the hallway toward the closed wooden door and heard Beltram on the telephone. Treehorn reached for the doorknob, and Raven knew without being told to back up his partner. The agent turned the knob and they entered the den.

"Maria, I told you I didn't want to be—"

"—disturbed?" finished Treehorn as his weapon aimed at Robert Beltram.

"I have two FBI agents pointing their guns at me. You're my lawyer. Deal with it." Beltram raised his voice and slammed the phone down.

"Robert Beltram, please stand and show us your hands. You're under arrest for the murder of Darcy Clearwater," Treehorn ordered as he came around one side of the desk while Raven took the other side.

Beltram didn't move instead he removed his Cuban cigar from the ashtray and took a puff until the end glowed red. His exhale filled the office with its rich aroma.

"Have a seat while I wait for my lawyer to return my call. I have the right to one call, correct?"

Treehorn could see the manipulative wheels turning in Beltram's eyes. "We have time for you to talk to your lawyer, but before you do, let me read you your rights: *You have the right to remain silent. Anything you say can and will be used against you in a court of law. You have the right to an attorney. If you cannot afford an attorney, one will be provided for you. Do you understand the rights I have just read to you?*"

Beltram answered, "Yes."

"With these rights in mind, do you wish to speak to me?"

Beltram replied again, "Yes," and downed the last of his Scotch that was in a glass.

"Are you sober?"

"This is the only drink I've partaken of today. Let's have a hypothetical discussion while we wait for my outrageously expensive attorney to earn his keep."

Treehorn wondered why men always developed the gift of gab upon their arrest. "We welcome your confession."

Beltram paused, "This isn't a confession, but hypothetically, where did it go wrong?"

"When Nichelle Walters killed your wife."

"Don't mention that woman's name in my presence."

"Then, you committed a murder to cover-up your crime."

"Conjecture." Beltram puffed his cigar.

"Darcy told me after you killed her."

"That's utter nonsense."

"*Call FBI Agent John Treehorn* is what she wrote."

"Why call you?" the CEO asked sarcastically.

"Let's start at the beginning and I'll tell you why." Treehorn spoke and they listened.

"The night of the murder you telephoned Darcy at the Missing and Murdered Indigenous Women's Movement dinner. You two argued. She drove to her apartment. You knew your son wouldn't be there. What you didn't know was that Darcy had picked up a witness who accompanied her home. You threatened her again, by telephone, and at that point she transferred her files from her computer to

287

her password-protected phone. You arrived there, argued again, and struck her with your left hand. Signing the letter at your office threw me off your trail for a short time, but Darcy pointed me back."

"How could a dead woman do that?" Beltram scoffed.

"The *Indian Times* on Darcy's bulletin board showed me your motive for murder and your capability for it."

"How so?" Beltram examined his manicured nails.

"The water contamination and that you're ambidextrous. Darcy realized you were dumping fracking contaminates at Granite Ridge. Her computer held the proof, and she transferred that file to her phone the night you killed her."

"Please proceed. I'm fascinated with your investigative skills." Beltram mocked.

"Did your employee inform you that the FBI executed a search warrant here yesterday when you weren't home?"

"No, but my lawyer would be interested in examining it."

"Oh, trust me, it was perfectly executed. I sent two agents to witness the fact."

288

Treehorn reached into his suit pocket and removed a sealed evidence bag like a magician conjuring the truth.

Beltram squinted at the bag labeled "EVIDENCE". "What did you plant?"

Treehorn ignored the dig. "It's the shard of glass from Darcy's watch. Bobby gave her the timepiece; a beautiful and expensive gift. She removed it only when she showered or slept. Did you know that it had GPS?" Treehorn didn't wait for a response. "It tracked her movements the day she died."

Treehorn watched Beltram's eyes as he processed that information. "When you stomped on her wrist the glass broke and became embedded in the sole of your brown shoe. My crime lab removed the glass under the warrant. It fitted perfectly into the crystal on Darcy's watch. Do you know the irony?" Treehorn asked. "You may have thought her time was up, but in actuality, your time was up."

Raven watched Beltram's facial expression change as he listened to the charges built against him. No amount of wealth would prevent his imminent arrest.

Treehorn replaced the first evidence bag with a second.

Robert checked his Rolex for the time. "Is that's all you've got, Mr. Treehorn?"

"It's *Agent* Treehorn. These two pieces of evidence will nail you for murder."

Robert glanced at the second bag. "What is it?"

Treehorn continued, "As you kept your weight on Darcy's wrist, you removed your wife's ring from her finger. The images from the MMIW dinner showed Darcy wore the ring before you killed her. The FBI lab recovered your partial fingerprints from it. The witness heard you say, 'No one misses you' but it was actually, 'No one Mrs. you.' stated in relation to the marriage to your son."

Raven watched as Beltram's face changed from rich white to pasty poor.

Treehorn continued his arresting statement, "You took a piss and that's when you flushed your life down the toilet, because you left your thumb print on the toilet tank lever."

"You haven't proved anything. I called my employee, stopped at her apartment, and used her facilities. She returned the ring to me because she knew it belonged to my wife. As for her watch, she told me she had broken it on the edge of her desk before I arrived. None of which are crimes."

"No, but you did kill her."

Raven watched and knew the handcuffs would be out soon.

Treehorn added, "You called Brody Hauler, who picked up Darcy's body. You removed her computer and left her apartment. You didn't have her phone. We have a printout of all the GPS locations from that night, Darcy's phone, computer, and her watch—which, by the way, tracked Brody's movement—your telephone and vehicle. You remember Agent Shelly? You spoke to him at Cookie Lighthouse's diner the night you killed Darcy. We tracked your GPS movements."

"Interesting theories about what I, and my employees do, after work hours."

"The GPS data tracked Darcy's computer to your office."

"That's good to know, Mr. Treehorn. I'll have my staff search the office again to locate where Darcy left it. She must have swung by her office the night she died."

"No, but she did swing by Granite Ridge the day she died." Treehorn watched as a flush appeared on the CEO's fleshy cheeks.

Beltram smirked. "Darcy conducted environmental work, Mr. Treehorn. I didn't micromanage her."

Raven watched the rich man spin his web of lies.

"When did you find out that Bobby and Darcy had gotten married?"

"It's a small town. There are no secrets here."

"Tell me about your son, Brody Hauler," Treehorn asked, but didn't believe Beltram would answer.

"A bastard to a whore I knocked up. She refused an abortion and disappeared with my wallet's cash before I could have my seed scraped out of her. Sixteen years later the kid showed up at my doorstep badly beaten and abused carrying a birth certificate that listed me as his daddy."

Treehorn let the suspect continue unabated.

"He informed me he buried his mother, alive, in an unmarked grave beneath a tree and hung her red dress on the limb to mark her as missing and murdered. As for his stepfather, Brody told me he cremated the man alive. He told me his only crime was being my bastard. I took pity on the boy, gave him a job, but he had to earn my loyalty first."

Raven knew the killer's next words would cause him to have nightmares.

Whereas, Treehorn lived with the horrors of men, "What did you ask of him?"

"My wife was dead. Nichelle Walters, the drunken Indian who killed my wife, lived a life of sobriety. Well, at least she did until the day Brody caught up with her in a

292

parking lot. He told me he kidnapped her, took some sexual liberties, and then drove her in her own automobile to the exact location where she murdered my beloved wife, Brenda. Brody filled her with my very expensive Scotch until she drowned in it. I gave him a red truck every year as a reward."

"Where is he?" Treehorn asked.

"I call him when I need him," Beltram smirked.

"How many women have you killed?" The smirk disappeared with the agent's question.

Raven watched a guilty man acquiesce at his guilt.

Beltram knew he was a dead man, not for murders he committed, but for what Agent Treehorn had unknowingly stumbled upon.

"I never kept track, Mr. Treehorn." He had nothing to lose now but his life.

"*Agent* Treehorn. How many did Brody kill?"

"I have no idea. Ask him when you find him."

"I have a feeling we're not going to find him. I think he's dead, and I think you killed him."

"My lawyer will deal with your slander."

"Where's Hanna Redmond?"

Beltram avoided eye contact with Treehorn. Instead of answering the agent's question he took one last drag of the cigar and snuffed it out in the glass ashtray. "I have no idea who that is."

"Liar," Treehorn thought. "Darcy Clearwater was pregnant with your grandchild," The agent stated for the record.

Beltram huffed, "Thank God she's dead so I won't have a half-breed in my family."

Raven watched as his friend flinched and wondered if the CEO had a death wish.

"Who kidnapped and killed Sandy Begay? Brody or both of you?" The agent grilled him.

"That skank? A worthless Indian whore in our throwaway society. She wasn't good enough to spread her legs beneath me."

Treehorn pursed his lips and ordered, "Stand up! You can call your lawyer from jail."

Beltram stood as Treehorn removed his handcuffs from his belt holder.

BOOM! The shotgun blast blew a cavity in Beltram's chest as the force of the pellets slammed his body back against the oak-paneled wall, where he slid down until his rear end hit the floor. Blood and body tissue colored his pristine white shirt, red.

"She was my cousin!" Kaya Massey screamed.

Raven wrestled Beltram's prized shotgun out of her hands before she could fire a second round. The gun's recoil had struck her face and blood from her nose spotted her Williston Cleaning Service uniform.

The Fed knelt down and listened to the murderer's final words: "Truth, it's buried, and you'll never find her." Beltram wheezed as his blood oozed from his mouth.

Treehorn spoke the last words the dying man heard, "Yes, but I'll be alive to search."

The FBI Agent, born half Navajo and half white, watched as the man's spirit left him. He didn't offer a prayer for the man, but for the women he killed.

The agents waited in the living room for the arrival of Buckman while the FBI crime lab conducted their investigation.

Treehorn's fingers tapped a rhythm on his thigh. "We've missed something."

"It's Buckman's problem, not ours," Raven stated. He thought of his wife and kids.

"Why kill Dennis Donovan?"

Raven knew Treehorn wouldn't stop. "Did he know something that someone wanted kept quiet?"

CSU Wilkerson walked past the doorway and Treehorn waved her over.

"Wilkerson, what do you know about those one hundred-dollar-bills given to Janie Nettles by Donovan?"

The CSU tech eyed the room to make sure no one else was listening and whispered, "You didn't hear this from me. They belonged to a dead DEA informant connected to the Mesa Cartel. There are rumors of money laundering across the Mexican border into Arizona and New Mexico. Who do you think has the power to hide billions of dollars outside the US and launder the money back inside this country?"

Treehorn answered before Raven, "The CIA."

"Like a said, you didn't hear it from me. Type your number into my phone."

Treehorn did as she asked.

The CSU clicked her phone and the pictures of the five $100-dollar-bills appeared with their serial numbers. "Those bills disappeared from an unsecured evidence locker when Donovan was murdered. Someone wants whatever's going on with the money to be buried." The CSU tech forwarded another image. "I sent you Donovan's crime scene photo with the five bullet holes that struck him. It's an assassin's signature. Find that shooter, and I suspect you'll find your answers."

Treehorn and Raven examined the image.

"Delete my number right now and I suggest you save that file elsewhere."

Treehorn completed Wilkerson's request.

The two agents continued to wait for Buckman's arrival. He observed Beltram's collection of trophies in the room. Expensive paintings of beautiful women, first edition novels, and classic sculptures filled the bookcases and cabinets. The most striking item in the room was a diamond and ruby necklace that gave the illusion of rippling blood and water as the sunlight struck it.

Treehorn reflected on the investigation, on Roni Allen's words about Hanna Redmond dating a Lakken employee, on Agent Garrand's conversation in the taxi about Brody assaulting a red-headed woman, and on Trooper Allen's offhand comment that people with money can hide any crime. Mysteries woven, rugs never finished.

Treehorn turned to Raven, "Thirsty?"

Raven nodded.

Agent Garrand finished his interview with Maria and Luis. "You're free to leave. We'll contact you if we have any further questions."

Treehorn asked, "May I have a glass of water?"

Maria smiled and handed him a clean glass from a cabinet. "Of course. And you?" she looked at Raven.

The younger agent nodded, "Please."

She turned on the faucet and the pressure dropped. "That happens a lot. We just wait for it to rebuild. You'd think an expensive house would have better water pressure."

Treehorn looked at Raven. "Check and see if water's being used upstairs."

Raven rushed to the stairs and searched the bathrooms. None of the CSU staff used any plumbing. He returned to the kitchen. "No one."

"Agent Garrand, recheck all of the outside buildings." The man rushed outside on Treehorn's orders.

Raven asked the gardener, "Where's the plumbing system?"

Luis pointed toward the rear of the house.

The agent requested, "Take me there."

Treehorn questioned Maria. "Does this house have a cellar?"

"Yes, it's Mr. Beltram's wine cellar and storage area for his Scotch."

"Show me!"

Chapter Eighteen

Dr. Ryder wheeled Robert Beltram's black body bag past Treehorn as the agent followed Maria to the cellar entrance. He removed his pistol from his holster. "Stay here."

The agent turned on the lights and started his search. The cellar was comprised of three rooms: a utility room with heating, air conditioning, and plumbing; a movie viewing room, recently used; and a massive wine cellar with bottles of wine stacked floor to ceiling on three walls. Crystal glasses on a testing table sat neatly arranged in the center. Nothing out of the ordinary for a rich man's worth, but Robert Beltram was rich and a murderer.

Treehorn continued his search. Along one wall cases of imported Scotch stacked neatly in their expensive custom-designed shelving unit that prevented any deterioration for his prized possession. The agent holstered his weapon.

Treehorn turned toward the door when a metal set caught his eye. He examined it in closer detail. A single key ring with three keys hung from a hook. That wasn't unusual; one key appeared to belong to a basic deadbolt and the other a small padlock key. It was the third key Treehorn's eyes zoomed in on. Every law enforcement officers identified with it and they all carried one, agent included: a handcuff key. Treehorn lifted the keys off the hook and showed Raven as he joined him.

They searched the room until they found the hidden deadbolt lock. Treehorn inserted the key, and the tumblers aligned to unlock the steel, soundproof door.

Two agents, guns aimed; one suspected the truth, the other didn't want the memory.

It wasn't a storeroom, but a prison. Though a lavish prison.

"FBI, show us your hands."

A red-haired woman sat in an ornate chair. Her floor-length, red velvet dress covered her from neck to her slipper-covered feet that peeped out from beneath. She raised her hands as two tears streamed down her face when she saw their FBI embossed vests.

"Hanna Redmond?" Treehorn asked.

She nodded and whispered, "Yes."

"Are you alone?"

Hanna nodded again.

Treehorn holstered his pistol. "John Treehorn, Raven Shelly."

Raven secured the adjacent room while his partner helped the woman.

"Let's get you out of here. Can you walk?"

She responded by lifting her dress. A metal handcuff wrapped her ankle, its other end connected to an elaborate floor rail system which clearly controlled her movements.

Treehorn knelt down and used the specialty key to unlock it. He held his hand out for her.

She grasped his hand as if it were the last lifesaver at sea. Hanna closed her eyes as she stood because she didn't want his expression to be forever engrained in her memories of this day.

Treehorn's ancestors would have been proud. His face remained stoic as he helped the pregnant woman from the chair.

"Get a blanket," Treehorn ordered Raven, who swiftly found one folded over a chair. The agent wrapped it gently around her. His act of kindness almost broke her resolve to stay strong.

"Do you want to feel the sunshine on your face?"

302

Hanna smiled as more tears filled her eyes and ran down her face.

Raven went first to clear a path. Treehorn felt the shock shake her body. He lifted her into his arms and held her tight as he climbed the steps.

Buckman's arrival coincided with Treehorn's exit from the mansion. He used his shoulder and shoved her aside as he passed with the girl. "Hanna Redmond."

The FBI supervisor stared wide-eyed and opened mouth, horrified. "I didn't know," she stuttered.

"How could you not?" Raven snapped as he passed her in his rush to open the SUV's rear door.

Treehorn placed Hanna inside the SUV and fastened her seatbelt.

Raven's hand caught the keys that flew through the air. He knew the hospital without being told.

Treehorn climbed into the back seat and watched over the young woman.

As Raven drove, Hanna opened the window to feel the sunshine on her face and the wind in her hair. No one cared how cold it became inside the vehicle. She stared out as the landscape change from oil fields to prairie to the populated town.

Treehorn telephoned Samantha, "How soon can you get to the hospital's emergency room?" She answered satisfactorily. "We have a woman with us and her name's Hanna."

Raven focused on driving with their emergency lights on and siren off.

Treehorn whispered, "Your father searched for you since your disappearance."

Hanna's resolve broke and she burst into sobs that shook her thin frame. She reached for Treehorn's hand to latch onto because all she wanted to do was to throw herself from the moving vehicle.

He held her hand tighter as if he sensed her thoughts and handed her tissues.

She leaned closer to him so only he could hear and whispered, "He called me Brenda every day."

"He's dead and he'll never hurt you or another woman ever again." Treehorn whispered.

Raven's eyes met Treehorn's in the rear-view mirror, and by the anger in his friends face he knew if Beltram wasn't already dead, Treehorn would have made sure of it. No one spoke during the remaining time, each lost in their own thoughts.

Buckman telephoned the hospital ahead of the agent's arrival and arranged special care for Hanna.

Samantha waited with a female doctor and nurse in the heated entrance.

Treehorn helped Hanna into a wheelchair and pushed it through the emergency room doors.

Raven drove off as soon as everyone was clear of the SUV.

"Hanna, this is Dr. Samantha Reynolds. She won't be treating you, but she'll be by your side to support you."

"Hi, Hanna. You can call me Sam. This is Doctor Shelby and Nurse Ryan."

The two females nodded in greeting. Dr. Shelby pointed to a door, "Room Three is available."

Hanna examined Samantha's bruised face. "You look like you're the one that needs help."

Samantha smiled and pointed at Treehorn, "He saved me, too."

Hanna looked at Treehorn. "Thank you."

He gave her a little smile with a nod. The agent thought of Beltram and how easy he got off with death by shotgun.

Treehorn waited outside the room and watched as the hospital staff came and went. He sent a text to Leo

Mancuso updating him on the case and the ensuing media storm that would soon follow.

Raven returned a short time later with his passenger, Jasper Redmond. By the worried look on Jasper's face, he knew Raven had warned him what to expect.

The retired Fed stopped in front of Treehorn and held out his hand, "Thank you."

The agent stood and shook the man's hand. He pointed to Hanna's room. "Someone needs you."

Jasper nodded and knocked her door, "Poppy."

"Daddy!"

The sobbing of a father and daughter filled the area.

Samantha left them alone and closed the door to give them their much-needed privacy. She touched Treehorn's arm, "Can I talk to you alone?"

A nurse walking past informed Samantha they had a grieving room available and she pointed the pair to its location.

Samantha waited until the door closed.

Treehorn knew by the pained expression on her face it was bad news.

"Hanna dated a Lakken employee by the name of Roy Johnson. He took her to a well that was being shut down. He tried to pressure her into having sex and she refused.

He struck her. When she came to, Brody Hauler was there. He pushed Roy into a hole, assaulted Hanna, and put a bullet in Roy's head. Hanna passed out. When she regained consciousness, she was in Robert Beltram's prison."

Samantha watched as Treehorn clenched his fists.

"Also, this isn't Hanna's first pregnancy, it's her second. She gave birth to a set of twins a year ago. They were taken from her the day she delivered them."

"Write it up, have Hanna sign it, and forward it to Buckman. She can deal with it but email me a copy too."

Treehorn watched Samantha walk away. Their time here was coming to an end. There was one thing he had to do before leaving town.

Winston Brooks stepped down from his water truck as two police vehicles drove into his yard. One was FBI and the other the North Dakota State Highway Patrol.

Treehorn watched as Trooper Allen read the man his rights while Officer Maresca handcuffed his wrists and placed him in the rear seat of their cruiser. The agent let the local LEOs take credit for arresting Winston for running Treehorn off the road. He didn't want the credit, paperwork, or time delaying his departure from this town.

The agent stopped at his lodging, loaded his luggage into the SUV, and deposited the keys into the secure lockbox. He took one last look at Samantha's door and drove away.

Raven waited for Treehorn's arrival. His bags were packed and he was eager to return home.

Treehorn walked into their office. The bulletin boards contained all of the images of the women and investigative materials. Nothing was touched. He nodded towards the boards, "Why hasn't this been broken down and placed in boxes?"

"Buckman ordered it left up. She's assigned agents to work all of the cases and wants it all available for them. I've turned in my report to her. She wants yours as soon as it's completed."

"Did you include Beltram's GPS details after he left the diner?"

"No. It served no purpose." Raven answered.

"Call Dana. Tell your wife she'll be seeing us in a few hours."

"You're flying to the Rez?"

"Just for the night. I'll travel to DC tomorrow."

Raven didn't ask about Dr. Reynolds. He'd learn the details on the flight.

Treehorn meticulously typed the remaining section of his required paperwork and placed it in an envelope. He knocked on Buckman's door with his report in hand.

"Come in." When saw it was him, she ordered, "Close the door."

Once again Buckman observed the Special Agent as he stood to attention for the last time in front of her desk. He was still the epitome of the FBI, the suit with a tie, weapon, badge, and no longer a wedding ring on his left hand.

He dropped the envelope he carried on the corner of her desk. "There's my final report."

She didn't touch it. Instead, she handed Treehorn an envelope with her name embossed on it, "I submitted a Letter of Commendation for you to the Director. You did an outstanding job here."

"I don't want it. Are we done?" Treehorn's stance never wavered.

Buckman stared at Treehorn and remained silent.

The agent stared down at Buckman. He didn't move.

Buckman let the envelope fall to her desk and nodded her head towards the door.

He took his cue to depart this hell hole. As he grabbed the door knob he remarked, "I left one thing out of my report."

"What?" snapped Buckman.

"The fact that Beltram came to your house and screwed you after murdering Darcy Clearwater. His GPS showed his route." He opened the door and walked out.

Buckman pursed her lips, "Prick!"

Treehorn heard and kept walking.

Bobby Beltram's private jet carried the FBI agents towards Gallup, New Mexico as they sipped cold beers. Meanwhile, Bobby sat alone at the front sipping Scotch as he looked at his wedding pictures that were recovered from his wife's computer. He offered the agents a ride since he was en route to Darcy's funeral with her family.

"I saw Dr. Reynolds hang a red dress on the tree at Darcy's body dump site."

"She hung it for Brody Hauler's mother and all of the pairs victims. They're out there somewhere, buried in unmarked graves. She just wanted to let them know that they're not forgotten."

"Did you talk to her before we left?"

"Shut up Raven."

"I see you've moved your wedding band to your right hand."

Treehorn stood and grabbed another beer from the refrigerator and handed it to Raven. "Think about your wife while I grab some sleep."

Raven watched his friend walk away, alone, again.

Treehorn silently entered the spacious bedroom that was located at the rear of the plane. He removed everything except his T-shirt and boxers. His body relaxed on the expensive cotton sheets as he stared up at the ceiling of the jet.

"Hey, Mr. Special Agent Man, do you belong to the mile-high club?" Samantha asked as her hand caressed his abdomen.

He smiled.

Two months later.

Trooper Toby Allen drove past mile marker 223 and decided to turn around at the next locator as he drank his coffee and munched on Cookie Lighthouse's gingersnaps.

The radio was tuned to the national news: *"A shocking and gruesome crime out of a Baltimore suburb. Two detectives, Jimmy T. Irvine and Gerri Jackson, who have been under investigation for sexual assaults and destroying evidence, were both found murdered at the home of Detective Irvine. Their crimes had first been reported four years earlier by one of their victims, Dr. Samantha Reynolds. The FBI and medical examiner released a joint statement that the male officer had been castrated while the female officer also suffered genital mutilation. It is noted that both victims were alive while the knifing took place, and both suffered fatal hemorrhages. Police stated that a business card with two words, THE RAVEN, written in real gold was the only piece of evidence left at the scene. Federal officials released the crime details only after crime scene photos were posted by a social media outlet out of Mexico City."*

Trooper Allen asked out loud, "Who did they piss off?" then he saw the red dress swinging from the oak tree branch as he neared the turn-around. What he saw next made him think he needed to have his eyes re-examined.

A mangy wolf sat at the base of the tree, beneath the red dress as if he knew the cop would arrive. Like a dog holding a bone, but this time it was a wolf that had a really big bone in its mouth. The wild animal dropped it and ran, ran like someone chased him, again.

Trooper Allen notified dispatch of the wild animal sighting as he exited his car and successfully avoided the mud puddles, this time.

"Please let it not be a human remain." He voiced to himself as the wolf ran away.

It was.

Winston Brooks sped down the highway and saw Trooper Allen as he stood next to a tree with his police radio in his hand.

The fired truck driver pointed at the cop, "Marcia, there's the prick who arrested me. Damn that Brody and damn that Fed too!"

"Don't swear in front of them, Winston." Marcia turned towards the back seat and smiled at the red-headed twins. "When Uncle Brody turns up, we'll thank him again, for giving us these girls."

The mangy grey wolf sat on the knoll and watched as the car passed by carrying the two stolen sisters.

THE END

SHADOW DANCER (Book 1) *'A victim never forgets.'* A dead man's clue sends FBI Special Agent John Treehorn, to the Land of his People, the Navajo Indian Reservation, to hunt an elusive murderer named 'Shadow Dancer' the same Indian myth who once brought this decorated law enforcement officer to his knees.

INDIAN POSSE (Book 3) *'Justice, she'll never be denied.'* FBI Special Agent John Treehorn hunts a killer on the Navajo Indian Reservation who murdered two members of Indian Posse, a ruthless gang who hunts criminals who failed to pay their debts to society.

BAD PENNY (Short Read #1) FBI Special Agent John Treehorn investigates a murder of an Indian Posse member who was killed by a gun which has two sets of incriminating fingerprints and two Indian suspects who refuse to answer his questions.

www.dinahmiller.com (Book orders and merchandise.)
www.facebook.com/SpecialAgentJohnTreehorn/ (Fan Page)
Cover Artwork by Leonie Cheetham
www.facebook.com/leoniecheethamart/

Line Editor: Mia Kleve

Line Editor: Annie Darek Morgan

E-book formatted by www.word-2-kindle.com

Made in the USA
Lexington, KY
01 July 2019